LEVI ROOTS is a highly successful entrepreneur, cook, musician, and speaker, and a role model for those starting up in business. He gained widespread fame in 2007 after appearing on the TV programme *Dragons' Den* seeking funding for his Reggae Reggae Sauce. Levi's companies Roots Reggae Reggae Sauce Ltd, Levi Roots Reggae Reggae Foods Ltd and his Levi Roots brand have since expanded rapidly, launching a wide range of Caribbean foods. The sauce was named best new food product at the World Food Awards, 2009. Levi was listed in the business section of *The Power List 2010* as one of the most influential black people in Britain.

Levi's first cookbook, *The Reggae Reggae Cookbook*, published by Collins, was a great success. Next came *Caribbean Food Made Easy*, a TV tie-in for his popular prime-time BBC2 series of the same name. This was followed by *Food for Friends* and *Spice It Up!*, both published by Mitchell Beazley. Many of his delicious recipes are served at the Papine Jerk Centre, his popular restaurant in south London.

As a successful reggae musician, Levi has performed with James Brown, was friends with Bob Marley, has sung to Nelson Mandela, and was nominated for a MOBO award in 1998. His single 'So Out of My Mind' launched his roots reggae album *Red Hot* in 2009. In the same year he was named Entrepreneur of the Year by Urban Music Awards.

Levi spends many hours talking to children and students in schools and universities, to encourage and inspire them to believe in themselves and to fulfil their personal and business potential. He has received the GAP community award from the Jamaican High Commission for being a community champion and a positive role model for young people.

First published in Great Britain in 2011 by Mitchell Beazley,
an imprint of Octopus Publishing Group Ltd,
Endeavour House, 189 Shaftesbury Avenue, London WC2H 8JY
www.octopusbooks.com

An Hachette UK Company www.hachette.co.uk

Group Publishing Director Denise Bates
Senior Editor Sybella Stephens
Copy Editor Alison Wormleighton
Art Director Jonathan Christie
Designer Jeremy Tilston
Production Peter Hunt

ISBN: 978 1 84533 597 7
Printed and bound in UK

YOU CAN GET IT IF YOU REALLY WANT

Start your business, transform your life

LEVI ROOTS

Mitchell Beazley

CONTENTS

FOREWORD

"If business is the new rock and roll, then Levi Roots is Elvis Presley."
PETER JONES CBE

When I first met Levi Roots on *Dragons' Den* and he emerged singing and playing his guitar, I knew in an instant I wanted to work with him. As I listened to his pitch about his Reggae Reggae Sauce product, I could immediately see the potential, with the right support, business strategy, and access to key industry contacts.

But the real opportunity I saw was in Levi himself. I saw his passion and was impressed with his commitment and conviction, and with his previous efforts to make a go of building a business around his 'secret' recipe sauce. He made and bottled this in his kitchen at home, helped by his family, and then sold it in small numbers through a handful of retailers and at London's annual Notting Hill Carnival.

Like most pitches, there were weak areas in the business plan – not least in such things as manufacturing capability, distribution, and financial projections. But there was nothing that I felt I would not be able to resolve and develop by working closely together with Levi and giving him access to my team and resources. Above all, I saw the potential for a scalable range of products, with Levi at the centre as the perfect living, breathing, and enthusiastic Reggae Reggae brand champion.

He sang to the Dragons, "*Put some music in my food for me...*" and that was enough of an inspiration for me to envisage helping to build a Caribbean food brand around a category of products in major retail chains in the UK and globally. Not only that, but the sauce tasted really good, too.

A lot has happened since I made that investment in 2007, which will be known to people who have followed Levi's progress, much of it widely covered in the media. He is now well on his way to achieving his dream, with products that have become a phenomenal success. He is now in demand as a personality in his own right, with three successful Caribbean cookbooks to date – and his own BBC television series.

Anyone who has met Levi, or heard him speak, will know that his entrepreneurial journey, which I am delighted and proud to continue to be part of, offers great inspiration as well as valuable potential learning for others. It is a fascinating and engaging story, just like Levi himself.

Indeed, Levi is always quick to give generously of his time to support and help others – young and old alike. It was therefore no surprise to me to learn that he had decided to collect and document his personal business experiences, combined with advice from those who have worked closely with him, in this book, *You Can Get It If You Really Want*, and share it all with other budding entrepreneurs.

In my opinion, this is an essential read for anyone starting out in business, and for anyone running an established company who needs inspiration and practical advice to take their business to the next level.

Peter Jones CBE

GET READY
TO GET
STARTED

"Your future success depends upon the strength of your self-belief and the choices that you make."

LEVI ROOTS

As I look back to my roots – to the small boy in Jamaica, to the young man growing up in London with a passion for music, and to the successful market stallholder at Notting Hill Carnival just a few years ago – the title of this book "You can get it if you really want" sums up my belief that, no matter where you come from and whatever your start in life, anything is possible. Back then I had very little financial security. Today I still live in the same community and have the same friends that I had in those early days; however now my family is secure, I can drive the car of my choice, and I am comfortable. With success comes responsibility, and I take that seriously. The message I want to share is that your future success depends upon the strength of your self-belief and the choices that you make – each and every day

Entrepreneurs do more than run businesses. They first of all have a passion for what they do, a hunger for success, and the commitment and willingness to work very, very hard. I truly believe that you *can* get it if you really want – provided you try, try, try. And I have seen it happen: not only along the rocky path to my own good fortune, but also in the fortunes of others who are single-minded in their determination to achieve their goals.

This book has been written for all those who, like me, are driven to succeed, but may need some help along the way. My 10 steps to cooking up a successful business will take the mystery out of the way business works, help you to make good decisions, and encourage you to plan ahead and get expert advice. Most of all, I want to encourage you to do it your way – with your heart and soul, and full of self-belief.

THE POWER OF BELIEF

I always say to new entrepreneurs that the skill of being enterprising doesn't belong to the select few; we're *all* capable of running a business. It's the power of our focus and the strength of our self-belief that drive us forwards or hold us back.

If you have heard of Levi Roots, you may know how, as Levi the Dragon-slayer, armed with only my guitar, my dreadlocks, and my 'Reggae Reggae Sauce Song', I sang my way up the steps of the studio of BBC TV's *Dragons' Den* – and faced five business Dragons. Walking away with the enthusiastic backing of two experienced investors and the promise of £50,000, I thought my business future was made. But it was just the beginning. The story had started several years earlier, and I still had plenty of lessons to learn along the way. Since that time my two companies Roots Reggae Reggae Sauce Ltd and Levi Roots Reggae Reggae Foods Ltd, have both grown rapidly. I now own a 65 per cent share of my business, and future plans are being driven forward with the wise and experienced guidance of my tamest Dragon, Peter Jones. He has become a business ally and friend, as well as my mentor. More of that later.

There are dragons everywhere in business. They take on many guises. They may take the form of a bank manager who won't provide a loan; they may be friends or family who don't believe in your idea; they are the business associates who don't deliver on their promises; or they could be the voices inside your own head. I had faced many, many dragons before the ones I met on TV that day. To defeat them, the trick is to be prepared, to know what you want, and to understand which business and personal tools you will need before you take one step inside their den.

> Self-belief has power, and it will influence the choices you make – each and every day.

Every time you face a setback, there is a lesson to be learned and a skill to be gained. Those skills become the tools in the armoury that will safeguard you in battle the next time you enter the business arena. They build experience and help you to adjust your mind-set. Sooner or later you will succeed – if you listen, learn, and stay positive. The most important business weapons of all are: believing in your idea, remaining true to yourself, and developing a watertight business plan.

STAY TRUE TO YOURSELF

My first job after I left school in 1974 was doing engineering work for Selby Engineering, in a factory that was just across from where we lived in Tulse Hill, Brixton, south London. I was earning about £13 a week. I got paid on a Friday, and each week I would run home and give my mother my wages. I was so grateful to her for all she had helped me to achieve at school.

But during my early twenties I became a bit wayward. This was Britain in the 1980s: a period of high unemployment and the miners' strike; when the controversial 'sus' laws (which allowed the police to 'stop and search' and arrest you if they suspected that you might be thinking about committing a crime) fuelled tension on the streets that resulted in riots in Brixton and Toxteth in 1981, and again in Brixton in 1985. It wasn't hard to get into trouble as a young black man in those days. I ended up in the wrong place at the wrong time, and in 1986 I fell foul of the law – and as a result spent over four years away in prison.

It's not something that I am proud of but I was lucky because while I was inside I learned so much about myself and my true values, which had a huge and positive impact on my future choices. I was also very fortunate because while in prison on the Isle of Sheppey, north Kent, I met a volunteer called Theresa. She was the arts liaison volunteer and she truly helped me to turn my life around.

It is very important to know who you are and who you want to be: to understand that every choice you make takes you further towards or away from the life you dream of. Even though I was in prison, I found I had some important lessons to learn. Rather than bemoan my fate, I decided to use the time in a way that would expand my mind. Theresa introduced me to the works of William Shakespeare and to poetry, which had a great influence on me. Even then, I knew I enjoyed writing, and I was interested in creating a publication, so she encouraged me to launch a newspaper called *The Bird* as a way of giving the prison inmates a voice – on paper.

Theresa helped me to see that I could be who I wanted to be and that I could choose to put the mistakes of my past behind me. I was allowed to work on a voluntary basis with kids in a local school, and

I developed many new skills that were to serve me well when I got back into the outside world. I knew I could have been released early, had I admitted the crime I was accused of – but I knew I was innocent and, like many others who are falsely accused, my pride would not allow me to confess to something I had not done. Most importantly of all, I discovered that I could leave my old life behind me and start again as the true Levi Roots: the person I wanted to be.

Once out of prison, while concentrating on building my music career, I also had a whole series of businesses, from fashion to music to food – and eventually the sauce. Every venture taught me new lessons and took me closer to where I am today.

THE IMPORTANCE OF HAVING A VISION

My experiences in life have taught me many things, but the most valuable lesson of all has been learning the importance of having a vision, turning the vision into a practical plan, and then remaining focused on that plan. In the chapters that follow I will show you how to create a plan of your own, so that you can fire up your chances of making your business dream a reality.

There is a wise saying in business that there is no such thing as overnight success, and it's usually true. Knowledge and experience are gained one step at a time. But being fully prepared for good fortune when it taps on your shoulder will help you to reach your goals more quickly.

An entrepreneur respects the power of his or her own mind. The seeds of success are planted in your mind first, and, as those seeds grow into plans and actions, so the roots of your future success will strengthen. This process depends on your power to dream, to see your success in your mind before it happens. First you dream the dream, then you dream a plan of action, and finally you live that plan, in every moment of every decision. Staying true to your vision means that you will be ready to take inspired action when the time comes, with a plan that will take you to where you want to be – so that your dream *does* come true.

YOU *CAN* GET IT *IF* YOU REALLY WANT IT

There are no rules governing who can be a success in business. Anyone, anywhere in the world, can be a business person – with or without a successful education, although knowledge and self-knowledge are very important. It doesn't matter what you sell or what you choose to do – that is your business. You can be a refuse collector, a hairdresser, an accountant, or a cake maker; you can aspire to be a sole trader, run a local business, or be part of a nationwide industry. Everyone's vision of success is different, and everyone's idea of 'enough' will vary. There are no barriers to success – apart from the ones we create ourselves.

Even as a small child, I always had the sense that there was more to life than I was getting – and that I somehow deserved more. Even in those early days, I was dreaming boyish dreams about what I wanted to achieve and who I wanted to be.

If you dream your future, and *prepare* for the future that you want, you will recognize your moment when it presents itself – and you will be confident that now is your time. The potential for success is always in us. We are all born with unique skills and abilities. It's how we bring them out and which ones we choose to develop that count. I want everyone reading this book to know that you do have it within you to succeed. I will help you to navigate the path through your own Dragons' Den, so you can learn from my experience and avoid the more obvious obstacles along the way.

My mother always used to tell me, when you're running for a bus, don't get caught between the stops. It's a good piece of advice. She meant that if you plan ahead you will always be in the right place at the right time. If you're caught between the stops, you're in limbo land. There's nothingness there. You need to make sure that you get a head start – and that you finish well. It is never too early to get a head start in business by gathering the skills you need to be an entrepreneur.

> Get yourself ready to take that inspired action when your time comes. And it *will* come.

When I give talks I always try to spot the entrepreneurial trigger in the people who come up to me. Sometimes it is obvious – to them, as well as to me – while at other times they need me, or somebody else, to encourage them and draw those skills out of them. There is always a trigger; there is always a skill; there are always signs. I have written my book to help entrepreneurs to spot the skill and potential within themselves, so they can get *themselves* ready for that first business move – and then find others who can help them to gain the experience and knowledge they need to succeed.

Don't hold yourself back by worrying about mistakes. Every entrepreneur is a risk-taker on some level. Only by taking risks and learning will you find your way – and reach your bigger goals.

Get yourself ready to take that inspired action when your time comes. And it *will* come. We all get opportunities at some stage in our lives – but do we answer to their call? We do if we are ready and we know that we have a plan.

> We are not born with business skills – they are learned, and making mistakes along the way will be part and parcel of acquiring these essential money-making skills. It's a bumpy ride and you're going to love it!

THE VALUE OF GIVING BACK

I believe it's very important to find out who you are. Without that it is harder to find focus or motivation. The young Levi, who left Jamaica to live in England, used to be called Keith Graham, but he didn't know who he was. He lost his way at times and took a few years to find his real identity. It was the great reggae music coming out of Jamaica and the culture of Rastafari that inspired me to change. My role models were two people who have influenced a generation the world over: Bob Marley and Nelson Mandela. They inspired me to become the best I could be. Later on I changed my name to Levi Roots, and I left Keith Graham behind for ever – but that is another story.

> Inspiring somebody to dig deep in their soul to find personal qualities and strengths they didn't know they had is a powerful tool to have.

It's important to have yardsticks in life, to have something to aspire to, and to have somebody to look up to. At present my yardstick is the success of my five-year business plan, and my role model is my investor, Peter Jones. He can't sing and he still knows very little about reggae, but he is learning more about Jamaican food – and his business model lies at the heart of the success of the Reggae Reggae companies.

For me, one of the most satisfying things about the Reggae Reggae Sauce experience is that when people come up to me they don't just say, "Levi, I like your sauce" they use words like 'inspiration' and 'role model'. For my community, my success on *Dragons' Den* was about much more than Levi winning the investment. For once there was a black man on TV who was about to be successful in business, as opposed to being able to run fast or kick a ball.

I go about my business consciously, carrying that knowledge on my shoulders.

So this book is about giving back: to those who, like me, did not begin life with the best opportunities, but who have a hunger to succeed; and to others who have noticed the progression of the Reggae Reggae companies and just want to know how to create the best possible business. If I can inspire somebody to dig deeper, or to try harder, then I am grateful for the opportunity and the chance to do that.

Seeing other people do well is always motivating. I always get a lift when my football team does well or I see Usain Bolt win another gold medal for Jamaica – but the challenge is to *stay* motivated once that inspirational influence has disappeared. There is no point in waiting around for lady luck to help you out because she might get distracted and help someone else first. Waiting for luck wastes precious time. Your day may never come. Self-motivation is to do with making things happen and knowing where you are heading.

In the following chapters I will share with you all the knowledge I have gained over the course of my business ventures, to encourage everyone who is starting out to get motivated and to stay that way, as well as to keep an open mind, to ask many, many questions, and to ask for advice from those who have blazed a trail before them. It is an exciting time to be building a new enterprise, and you *can* do it… if you really want it. But you must *try, try, try – and try again.*

LEVI'S TOP 10 ROOTS OF SUCCESS

1   Feel the power of the p-word – passion
2   Know your market – and never stop networking
3   The plan is your key to success
4   Find yourself a mentor
5   Make yourself and your business special
6   Never be afraid to make mistakes
7   Surround yourself with like-minded people
8   Focus on finance
9   Stay true to your values
10 Be in it for the long term

LEVI'S BUSINESS JOURNEY

If you, like me, have taken an unconventional path in life, take heart from my CV (resumé), which tells a story of two careers - in food and music - several businesses, and a few hard lessons learned along the way. I have written about my early life in my *Reggae Reggae Cookbook,* and there will be more to come when I write my autobiography.

1958 Born Keith Graham in Clarendon, Jamaica.

1969 Moved to the UK to join family.

1970s

Worked for Selby Engineering. Warehouse manager for Magnet & Southerns timber yard and hardware store.

Joined team of Sir Coxsone Outernational Sound System. Changed name from Keith Graham to Levi Roots.

1980s

Became an MC for Sir Coxsone.

Formed reggae band, Matic16.

Set up production company, Conqueror Records.

Launched solo music career in Jamaica.

Set up Papine Pool Centre, Brixton, south London.

Ran prison newspaper, *The Bird*, while serving time on the Isle of Sheppey, north Kent.

Met Theresa, arts liaison teacher.

1990s

Started High Fashion Boutique, Acre Lane, Brixton.

Sang to South Africa's president, Nelson Mandela.

Mortgage advisor for Abbey National building society.

Sold rights in Conqueror Records to Kicking Records.

Started Levi Roots Rasta'rant at Notting Hill Carnival.

The Levi Roots Band on tour.

2002 Began recording studio album *Red Hot*.

Delivery driver for Parcelforce (took job to finish album).

2004–6 Worked at Plumbase plumbers' merchants, Brixton.

2006 Began selling the sauce with the name Reggae Reggae Sauce.

End July Approached GLE oneLondon for funding. Met Nadia Jones.

End August 4,000 bottles of Reggae Reggae Sauce sold in two days at Notting Hill Carnival.

Created Reggae Reggae Sauce business plan.

Applied for and received £1,000 for marketing and labelling.

November Approached by BBC's *Dragons' Den* researcher at the World Food Show.

2007

9 January Appeared on *Dragons' Den*. Sold 40 per cent of Reggae Reggae Sauce to Peter Jones and Richard Farleigh for an investment of £50,000.

February Reggae Reggae Sauce sold via 600 stores in an exclusive deal with Sainsbury's supermarket chain.

GAP award granted at Jamaican High Commission.

April Papine Jerk Centre opened in Battersea, south London.

2008

June *Levi Roots' Reggae Reggae Cookbook* published by Collins.

September Bought back shares from Richard Farleigh for £200,000 to increase personal shareholding in Roots Reggae Reggae Sauce Ltd to 65 per cent.

2009

June Birds Eye Reggae Reggae Chicken Chargrills launched.

August *Caribbean Food Made Easy* published by Mitchell Beazley.

Release of single 'So Out of My Mind' followed by launch of studio album *Red Hot*.

World Food Award for Best New Food Product 2009 for Reggae Reggae Sauce.

Four new table sauces and four cooking sauces launched.

October Named in business section of 'The Power List 2010: Britain's 100 Most Influential Black People' (J P Morgan).

Invited to No. 10 Downing Street to meet British Prime Minister Gordon Brown.

November Urban Music Awards 2009 for Entrepreneur of the Year.

December BBC TV series *Caribbean Food Made Easy* aired on BBC2.

2010

February Birds Eye Frozen Food products Reggae Reggae Burgers launched.

May Kerry Foods products Levi Roots' Chilled Caribbean Foods range (nine products) launched, with an exclusive deal with Tesco supermarket.

August *Food For Friends* published by Mitchell Beazley.

September Reggae Reggae Peanuts and Cashews launched.

On tour with the 'Levi Roots Experience'.

October Levi Roots Chilled Caribbean Meals shortlisted for two major food awards.

2011 *You Can Get It If You Really Want* published by Mitchell Beazley.

2012 onwards Plans afoot to launch in USA.

Dragons' Den is a television programme that allows would-be entrepreneurs to pitch their business idea to a group of fiery self-made millionaires in exchange for a tough grilling and the opportunity to win investment and business advice. My experience on the programme has become a part of my brand and my business story, and I am proud and grateful for that. *Dragons' Den* was a dramatic episode – but it was neither the beginning nor the end of my business adventures.

CHAPTER 1

WORKING OUT WHAT YOU WANT

Roots of success 1:
Feel the power of the p-word – passion

> *"There is no passion to be found in playing small – in settling for a life that is less than the one you are capable of living."*

NELSON MANDELA

You are never too young to start arming yourself with the necessary tools to become an entrepreneur. It is important to learn to recognize your talents and to make the most of your gifts; to care about what you are doing and to do it wholeheartedly.

Like many young people my first entrepreneurial venture started in the school playground. I used to sell individual biscuits from branded packs, setting different prices according to type and flavour. For instance, if I bought a packet at £1 and there were 24 biscuits in a pack, I would sell them to my friends for 10p or 20p each. I enjoyed doing it. It helped me to make my mark at my new school, and I liked the fact that I could get a return on my pocket money. Sometimes I would have a little munch in class as well – which didn't go down too well with my teachers. That was a lesson learned. Even in a commercial business, eating the stock is never a good idea; it will always get you into trouble!

Looking back, I think my first taste of business helped to feed my commercial instincts. If only I had thought to *make* the biscuits, too! My first business venture didn't develop far – but it was a useful lesson in selling, and perhaps that was when I first discovered my skill for turning food into profit.

YOU HAVE TO HAVE A PASSION

When people ask me whether their bright idea would make a successful business, I ask them first whether they believe in the idea themselves – and whether they have a plan. So much about success begins with a positive attitude of mind and structured approach.

To succeed in business, you have to believe in what you do and know what you want. It's all about that p-word – passion. This is the engine that drives you forward. It is the heartbeat, the crucial ingredient in your recipe for business success. In the initial stages of starting up your company, your passion will become an energy force that makes everything happen. It will drive you to become more than you realized you could be. It's a must in your start-up armoury.

People who are successful in business will see an opportunity and feel excited by it, where others may see only problems. Entrepreneurs often see the potential immediately, before they have all the details, but then are savvy enough to ask the right questions to make sure that the idea is sound.

If you're having trouble deciding what kind of business to set up, ask yourself first what you are good at doing and what you most enjoy, then consider whether there is a way you can make money from that skill. Next, imagine it is cold and raining, there is a train strike, and you have a 6am breakfast meeting. Would you still be motivated to get smart, stay sharp, go to where you need to be, and pitch your idea to potential investors or sell your product or service to a new customer? The only answer to any of these questions must be yes. There is no room for a 'maybe' in business. The question of profitability can come later. For now it is about discovering whether you have a passion for what you are going to do. It may seem an obvious thing to say, but you will always have trouble sticking to a long-term plan for a business concept that you don't believe in, dislike, or even hate. You have to believe in what you do.

Passion is important because it gives you the motivation and the reason to stay on plan for the long term. Whatever your plan is, make sure that it is something you enjoy doing because, after the initial buzz has passed, your passion for the idea will be the reason you stick to your plan.

Some people will go to university and study a subject such as law for five or six years, then, when they come out of university, they will end up working as, say, a bouncer or in a bar. Now that, to me, is a waste. If you have a real vocation and you enjoy your work, you need to find a way to make it happen then stick with it for the long term. It all contributes to the business recipe as a whole. The passion feeds into your plan as well as your commitment.

GETTING OUT OF YOUR COMFORT ZONE

My business story has its roots in music. I would not be here now if it hadn't been for my first career, in music. I was in the music world for 25 years or so. The truth is that I always thought I would make my money from music. It was my livelihood but I also stayed with it because I was enjoying myself. Music is, and has always been, my greatest passion, which is why I stuck with it for the long term. Sometimes in life, however, we discover that our main talent, or the things we most enjoy, will not make us enough money to support us.

Reggae has been a huge influence on my life. It shaped my development as I grew up as a young man, and I spent several happy years on the road, touring the world with Sir Coxsone Sound System. I enjoyed the lifestyle, and I was doing something that I loved. But I wasn't making a living; I was just getting by. I knew something had to change – but it took me a while to let go of what I knew. I was too comfortable to shake things up.

But I also had a secret weapon, which was my ability to cook. My wonderful grandmother Miriam Small had taught me about Caribbean cooking with herbs, spices, and using marinades to add flavour. She was my inspiration. I used to cook for family and friends, then in 1991 I opened up my Rasta'rant at London's Notting Hill Carnival.

Most entrepreneurs I know, including all five investors on *Dragons' Den*, have acquired their wealth outside the careers they trained and studied for. I didn't set out to develop a career in food, but over several years my reputation at the Carnival as a cook as well as a musician continued to grow.

> Sometimes we discover that the things we most enjoy will not make enough money to support us.

When I first started cooking my sauce, it was just for fun. It was a real family affair. I would cook it up in the kitchen – just me and my children. It would be impossible to get into my house from July until the end of August because the place was filled with jars, and everything smelled of herbs, pepper and garlic. We all loved to be involved. That passion has now passed on down the chain of supply to our customers.

Later, I began to put the bottles of sauce in a rucksack and walk around selling it at Brixton market. There was time to chat and to find out what was happening – and what was cooking. The place was brimming with scents and flavours.

My wake-up call came slowly. We had been building our reputation with the sauce since 1994, and the bottles ran out more quickly each year. But I was only paying partial attention.

In the meantime I had been enjoying my musical career. But the late 1990s were troubled times in Brixton, and reggae music was falling out of vogue in the music scene. The touring stopped and my musical career was on hold for a time. Early in the 2000s I worked as a delivery driver, and then came my low point. While I was working in a plumbers' yard, I hit rock bottom with nowhere to go. I looked at where my journey had taken me. I had gone from being a reggae singer touring around the world to working at a plumbers' yard, and I couldn't see my way back. It felt as if my spirits couldn't sink any lower. Even as a man of Rasta culture, I had lost faith. And the truth is, I got to the point where I felt so low I prayed for help. Not for the first time, I received it.

There is a popular saying: "When life hands you lemons, make lemonade." Well, my life was facing a lemon or two, and I was needing new inspiration. I had always had at the back of my mind the idea that my sauce was marketable, and now it came to me that *this* was the time to do it. The sauce was so much more than fizzy lemonade – I had the recipe for the sparkling champagne of Caribbean sauces. I already knew how to make it, I already knew that there was a market for it, and I knew that the market was growing every year. In that moment I knew that something else was going to happen. Other people will reach their realization in some other way, but I think my life changed from that point – because I started being able to focus on my vision. I was determined to make it work.

The next day I went into my manager's office and told him, "I'm going to be leaving the job to set up my own business. I'm going to be doing the sauce." I was full of excitement at the potential.

Later, I chose the name Reggae Reggae Sauce because it represents both music *and* food, and everything I am about. Had I decided to call it Levi Roots Scotch Bonnet Hot Pepper Sauce – or something like that – it might never have worked (or not on the same scale). The name of the sauce tells you everything about my path.

> One of the many things I have learned is not to get too comfortable. If we stop being alert to the marketplace, our competitors will steal a march and take our place.

INSPIRED ACTION

Learn to recognize the moment. It's known as 'inspired action': getting the inspiration, planning steps that will turn the inspiration into practical action, then taking that action... and not looking back. Once you have started, you need to maintain the momentum and keep that goal in your sights.

Inspiration comes easily to many people. They can have an idea a minute, or several per month. The thing is to find a way to keep the inspiration going – so that the ideas, the momentum, and that crucial energy force are not lost. For instance, you may wake up one day and think, "I feel like doing something for charity. I want to run a marathon." In fact, the percentage of people who *act* on a thought like that is quite small. You may get the inspiration to do something, but it becomes inspired action only when you are totally focused on your goal and have taken the first practical step towards it.

My philosophy is always to be ready for the next step in the plan, so that, when the moment presents itself it already seems familiar, and I can take action. If you are well prepared, there is no drama involved in making progress – because you have already seen yourself in that position. The trick is to recognize when it is *your moment* to take action.

People ask me what I would have done without *Dragons' Den*. In fact, I had been associated with food and with my Rasta'raunt since 1991: 15 years before my tame Dragons came along, so I believe I would have continued to make my sauce and to pitch it to distributors and suppliers. It would have taken me much longer, and I would have made more mistakes doing it my own way – but the moment when I decided to get out of my comfort zone and do the sauce was my moment of inspired action.

Put some music in your food

Deciding to step away from my ambition as a musician to focus on developing the sauce was a major decision for me because music is a big part of who I am. I love it and had always expected to make my name through music in some way. At first I thought I had to make a choice: to put the music down to rest, and bring the sauce forward. But then I realized that the two were linked – through me. There would be no sauce without Levi and no Levi without music. So, long before any hint of a TV programme, I decided to write my song as a way of defining my purpose for myself.

The 'Reggae Reggae Sauce' song says clearly, "This is me. This is Levi. Music and food. You can't separate the two." And that is my USP, or Unique Selling Point – the minute you pour the sauce, you will remember the song. Many will recall the moment on *Dragons' Den*… they will think of Levi… and they will remember everything about who I am. In that moment, it is the Levi Roots song and the brand that they are buying – not just a sauce.

All Dragon-slayers need a magic shield and sword before they venture into the unknown to slay dragons – and that is the purpose of a USP. It is a valiant weapon of protection against an unknown foe. My shield and sword were my guitar and my 'Reggae Reggae Sauce Song'.

I knew that the Dragons would be intrigued from the moment that I put my foot on the stairs and started singing. It was a pitch that made a bold statement about my culture, too. In Jamaica music is in the soul of the people and at the heart of everything we do. It is everywhere. I always say that Jamaicans make a song and dance about everything: we literally do. In Britain people ask me why I wrote a song about my sauce, but in Jamaica it would be crazy to think, "Levi has a sauce and he hasn't got a song to go with it," especially as I am a singer as well.

The song and the name are what made my sauce different. If I had just turned up with a bottle of sauce, wearing my best suit, and had told them that it was based on a home-grown recipe, the Dragons would have had me for breakfast. But my approach and my pitch were unique. No one had ever done that before – and that's what you need, really. To be genuine and to be different.
That is the true purpose of a USP.

Commitment

When I decided to commit myself 100 per cent to developing the sauce business, I also committed 100 per cent to selling the concept and building my brand. When you go into something for the long term, you've got to have a reason to stick with it. We all remember what it felt like as a kid to go into a store knowing that you finally had enough cash to buy something you had your heart set upon. That feeling never really goes away. I still get a buzz of excitement knowing that I am about to spend my hard-earned cash on something I have had my eye on. But the truth is that if the person who is serving you doesn't have the passion to sell it to you, the company may lose that sale. You may still want it, but if the person in front of you doesn't seem to care, you're likely to decide to take your business somewhere else. The passion has to resonate through from the beginning of the development to the end point of the sale.

My passion for what I do is the reason that the business Dragons invested in something they wouldn't usually have gone for. Strumming my guitar and singing my song told the Dragons, "I believe in my sauce, and I'm literally singing its praises. You had better believe it, too." It's a good thing they did – before I went on the programme, my kids had warned me, "Dad, you're risking everything by singing that song live on TV." In my community there is no coming back from loss of face.

> Your passion is an energy force that, when focused, will supercharge your progress. It will ensure that you get off to a strong start and help you to maintain momentum – all the way to the finish line.

Your passion will ensure that you get off to a strong start and help you to maintain momentum. In business, this means many things. At start-up stage it means being driven to get every aspect of planning your business right and not allowing yourself to become disheartened by the setbacks; having the stamina to work long hours and being willing to forfeit time out while you get your project up and running; making adjustments when things go wrong, so that you do things better next time; and planning and rehearsing every detail, so that you deliver an excellent result.

Passion will deliver the business you want and also provide the stamina to keep you going beyond the excitement of the start-up phase of your business race; through the exhaustion and the challenge of the middle laps; and onwards to the finishing line and your launch date. At the beginning of the start-up phase, you're always accelerating. You're at your most powerful – trying to give everything of yourself. That energy force will keep you going right through to the point where you get a genuine taste of success.

> The bottom line is that, to succeed in business, you have to believe in what you do. It's all about that p-word – passion. Passion is the engine that drives you forward. It is the heartbeat, the crucial ingredient in your recipe for business success.

COMMIT TO YOUR IDEA

Creating a business concept is similar to making music.
No one really makes *new* music because so much has
already been created; it is about being inspired by what
has been developed in the past, then adding to that and
creating something that is unique to you. Dub it up, mix it up,
and make it your own. Business ideas, too, can come from
anywhere. It is not so much reinventing the wheel as taking
something that already exists and remixing it into your own
version. A new business venture is often an extension of what
is already in the marketplace.

Every business idea fulfils a desire or a need. It may
be a product or a service; a franchise or a licensing
arrangement. It may do something better than the version
that came before, or it may create a new business niche
(such as building the market for Jamaican food and
launching a tasty hot pepper sauce, for example!). Don't
try to do too much at once. Keeping your business model
simple will make your life so much easier, and give you a
greater chance of success.

There may be no such thing as a *new* idea, but there
are plenty of good ideas. The challenge is to make sure that
the one you invest in is something you feel motivated by
and that is commercially viable. You don't know whether
your idea would work? I will share with you my business
experience and the value of networking and market
research. Lacking in self-confidence? Don't let that stand in
your way. We all gain confidence from learning and trying
new things. Too proud to ask others for their feedback or

their help? You might want to take a look at that. No man is an island, and no business is either. Thinking you know it all – or even that you *need* to know it all – will slow down your progress. I believe that everyone has it within them to make a success of something that they care about, but it means setting your thinking to permanent 'can-do' mode.

Business owners need to lead from the front if they are to inspire others to invest, follow, or buy. The important thing is to believe in what you do. You might be telling me you have a great business, but, if you don't believe it, I'm not going to believe it – and when you approach a potential investor, the answer will be no. It's important from the outset to develop an idea you truly believe in because one day that idea is going to be a product or service that you have to sell.

> A new business venture is often an extension of what is already in the marketplace.

KNOW YOUR USP

Know your USP, or unique selling point. This is probably my favourite business tip of all. It is the element of your business, service, or experience that is individual and special, and makes you stand out from the crowd. It is crucial. Before going on *Dragons' Den*, I had never heard the term 'USP', but, as soon as it was explained to me, it made perfect sense – and, in fact, summed up what I was about.

Since then, 'Know your USP' has become a central topic in my talks. You have to know what it is, especially if you are launching a new product or idea. If you don't know what is unique about what you are offering, how will you communicate it to others and how will anyone know whether they want or need it? Your USP is personal to you or your product. It's the special bit in the business plan, the shiny part – like the cherry on top of the cake. It stands out, and it belongs only to you.

> Your USP is personal to you or your product. It's the special bit in the business plan, the shiny part – like the cherry on top of the cake. It stands out, and it belongs only to you.

For a business start-up, knowing the USP is the vital thing. You have to have one right from the 'get go'. As soon as you've thought of your idea, follow up with the questions, "What is at the core of my purpose? What is it that I'm *really* going to sell?" Until you know the answer, you aren't ready to run with your idea.

A business may also benefit from a mission statement or from a vision statement, but those are more strategic. A mission statement describes a company's purpose; a vision statement describes the company's future. Neither is as personal as your USP. There will be many times in your business life when you will have three minutes or less to make an impression on someone who can have an impact on your business. Your USP can get the point across in moments.

There is another important p-word in business – pressure. There is a lot of it about, and it is a big consideration. There will be tough times and challenges; days when you face nothing but problems; and periods when your sales and cash flow are going down instead of up. You need to know that you can handle the pressure, otherwise there will be no joy in your achievements.

> It's no good saying you want fame and fortune if, when it comes to it you don't care to wear those shoes.

WHAT'S DRIVING YOU TO SUCCEED?

There are as many reasons for being in business as there are people in business. Your reasons for working long hours, very hard, not always for much in the way of financial return (in the early days), are personal to you. But it is important to know yourself well enough to understand what *is* driving you to succeed. In my case, my main priority is creating financial comfort and security for my family.

I hadn't really known my mother before I came to England. My parents had left Jamaica when I was still small, to try to build a new and better life for our family. We were apart for several years before they sent for me, and in the meantime I had formed a strong bond with my grandmother, who looked after me back home in Jamaica, until I was 11. My mother and I had both missed out on those crucial early years, so we were getting to know one another again.

For the first year after I arrived in the UK, I struggled at school – not just in English because I couldn't get the language right, but across the board. As a result, my mother began to tutor me at home in the evenings. Years later she admitted that she was re-educating herself when she was teaching me. She had to stay one step ahead the whole time. But she was the most fantastic teacher. As well as English and history and mathematics, she taught me the value of money – how to manage it and the importance of saving it – together with other business insights. She got me books so that I could concentrate, and helped me to catch up in school. I could not have gotten through my schooldays without her help.

Giving her my early biscuit takings from my school business venture, and later on my early wage packets, was really my way of saying, "Thank you for bringing me through, even when I couldn't focus in school." It was a formative time, feeding the determination to succeed that is still within me. It can take as much effort to do something small as to achieve something large, so you might as well dream and plan as large as you can.

My mother and my seven children are my main motivation to succeed. My mother is now in her eighties, so it is time for me to look after her. There's an old Jamaican saying: "Once a man, twice a child." If I want my children to be in a position to look after me when I am a child again, I had better dream as big as I can!

YOU CAN LIVE THE DREAM

You *can* have it if you really want – but you have to *really, really* want it – and you have to plan for it as well. Sometimes, when I stress to people that building a business is not easy, that they have to plan and work hard from day one, they begin to think, "I don't want that kind of high-pressure life." And that's fine. Better to know yourself and stop before you get started than to embark on something that is really not for you.

But the way I look at it is this: because you've worked hard for it, in the long run you're really going to enjoy what you have created, suffered for, and worked for. To be a success you really do need to make your work and your business not only your passion, but also your purpose. So start cooking up your research, and plan your business menu now.

CHAPTER 2

WHAT'S STOPPING YOU GETTING STARTED?

**Roots of success 2:
Know your market –
and never stop networking**

*"Be true to yourself and
you will get the best from you.
Self-denial stifles growth."*

LEVI ROOTS

What will stop you from getting your business started? Nothing – if you feel passionately enough about your idea. What *should* stop you from getting started? Two things: not having enough market knowledge and not having a strong business plan. You need to get to know your market inside out before you launch your venture. Set out to gain as much knowledge as you can: about your product, your market, your suppliers, your competitors – and yourself. This knowledge is the second weapon in your Dragon-slayer's armoury. Once you understand your market and your territory, you can create a business plan that will be 'fabulocious' – and a true recipe for success. (The plan is coming up in Chapter 3.)

You can learn about your industry in many ways:

- From a business mentor, who will share their insights and experience
- From personal contacts and experience of working in the industry
- By networking and information gathering – the surest way to get yourself known in the business, while you find out what's really happening

When you build your business on facts, you feel more confident – and your clients, customers, and potential investors are more likely to respect your wisdom. Never assume what people want or guess the size of the market: you need solid information to act upon. Passion without knowledge can be hot-headed and unfocused, and may lead you to act without insight. You can never know too much – although to get started you just need to know 'enough'.

> Passion without knowledge can be hot-headed and unfocused, and may lead you to act without insight. You can never know too much – although to get started you just need to know 'enough'.

KNOW WHAT YOU DON'T KNOW

Don't try to pretend that you know more than you do. Self-denial stifles growth. It can lead you to do things the hard way, and slow down your progress. Instead, take advantage of the wide resources and sources of advice that will be available in your local area, and do everything you can to test out your business idea. Your time is precious, and you may never have the luxury of having enough space to learn the basics again.

Developing the skills you need is all about educating yourself about the ingredients your business needs to succeed. The start-up phase is a good time to do a 'SWOT analysis' of your newly formed idea: focusing on the Strengths and Weaknesses, looking at the Opportunities it presents, and considering all the Threats (from competitors, lack of cash, lack of time, and anything else that crosses your mind). This is useful because it helps you to see what you have, as well as what you need.

You can do a SWOT analysis of yourself, too. What are your own strengths, weaknesses, opportunities, and threats? For example, if you are setting up a business that involves selling goods online, but you don't know much about computers, that is a weakness. You need to bring yourself up to speed and learn all you can. Taking an evening class would be a good idea.

When I appeared on *Dragons' Den*, it was pretty clear to everyone watching that I needed to learn how to read a balance sheet and to get my finances straight. That was my Weakness. On the other hand, my Strength was my sales and marketing skill. I know I am a great salesman; I think I could sell anything to anyone. The Opportunity was the programme. The Threat was that the Dragons might say no. These days I have got to grips with the finance, and I work closely with my finance team, so my SWOT analysis looks different. It will change again when we take the brand to new countries and territories because what is seen as a strength in one arena may not be in another. The needs of your business will change over time, and that is why you need to know who you are and be ready to adapt to what the market needs from you.

A SWOT analysis is usually laid out in a matrix, for example:

Strengths	Opportunities
Weaknesses	Threats

My personal SWOT analysis

Strengths

- Music
- Integrity
- Focus
- Delegation and trust

Music: Music and Levi go hand in hand, which is why I love what I do. I have managed to merge the things I enjoy most, and that is why business is so much fun for me. It is a unique way of doing business, and I never find it boring because it allows me to work hard and to enjoy what I do.

Integrity: If you are synonymous with your brand, you have to be ready to be on show the whole time. I am comfortable in my own skin, so it is usually straightforward for me to stay true to myself and present a consistent face to the public.

Focus: I am a hard worker. The desire to hold on to what I have and to stay successful keeps me on track and my foot on the accelerator.

Delegation and trust: When you are learning as quickly as I have had to, you know you can't do it all yourself. I have built an excellent team who have strengths that complement my own.

Weaknesses

- One-man brand
- No big business experience
- Limited finances

One-man brand: When you are a one-man brand, everything relies on you, and you can't put a foot wrong.

Everyone loves you because you are new, but that means you are also vulnerable to fashion or tastes changing. However, when you become successful you may come across people who will try and knock you back down. The only solution is to be yourself, whomever you are working with.

No big business experience: I've run several small businesses before but I wanted to take this business to the next stage. I did my homework and had the self-belief that I could do it.

Limited finances: When I started selling Reggae Reggae Sauce I really had no money at all. I had to prove that I had a business before I could go off and raise investment.

Opportunities

• Brand expansion

• Expansion into new territories

• Personal influence and new projects

Success brings new opportunities. As your company grows, you will find that new doors open to you. Because I have worked hard, chances are now coming my way that enable me to use all of my talents. These include things that I would not have been considered for in the past. When you create your own change, you will be given the chance to shine.

Threats

• The unknown or illness

As we say in Jamaica, "If you wan' be good, your nose has to run." You have to work hard and stay healthy, and keep looking over your shoulder – because nothing is for ever.

SWOT ANALYSIS FOR THE REGGAE REGGAE SAUCE BRAND

Strengths
- Integrity
- Feel-good association
- Personal story
- Taste

Integrity: The strength in the brand lies in its association with me and the integrity of who I am and what I stand for.

Feel-good association: It is a brand associated with a positive attitude and fun.

Personal story: Those who know my story will also know that if a lone Rasta man wearing a guitar around his neck can achieve what I have done with the Dragons' help, then anyone can do it. "You can get it if you really want it."

Taste: No food product will survive unless it tastes good. Ours tastes great and has stayed true to the original flavour.

Weaknesses
- Newness
- One-man brand
- Very fast growth

We have potential weaknesses but, because the brand is built on solid foundations and is supported by an excellent team, they are not active weaknesses at this time. The brand is very new, so it is still dependent upon me as the figurehead. We are quite a way off its becoming a Kellogg's or a KFC, where the brand is so long-established that the founder is no longer needed for its success to continue with the name alone.

Opportunities

- New products/brand expansion
- Consolidation in the UK
- Expansion overseas

We are in the happy position of being out in front of the Caribbean food market, blazing a trail for others to follow. The exciting thing is that the opportunities ahead are not only for the Reggae Reggae Group of companies and our brands, but for other Caribbean products as well. If we are trying to 'big up' the world pool of Caribbean food, the more players there are in it, the better. The bigger the niche, the more attractive the market becomes worldwide – and the better for all of us.

We are now creating opportunities to expand the brand outside the UK. We've stuck to our 5-year plan, we have created and built up the brand in that space of time – and now we have to replicate that model in the international market, over the next five years.

Threats

- Health and safety issues
- Competition

The main threat to any food brand comes in the form of health and safety-related issues. We take the quality of our food-production process very seriously.

The last thing any food manufacturer wants is for something unwanted to turn up in a sauce bottle. If you are selective about your business partners and make sure that you work with the best, you will protect yourself in the best way possible against the threats.

The other threat, which is common to almost all businesses, is that our competitors are chasing us fast – and our success makes it easier for them to catch up and follow.

KNOW YOUR TERRITORY

Knowing your territory is vital in business. Until you know your sector of the market inside out, you can't begin to make your mark or know how best to reach your customers.

If you like to cook, you will know how good it feels to stir things up in the kitchen – confident that your family, friends, and guests will enjoy your food because you know *exactly* what they like to eat. You can be sure that they will be back for more, and telling all their friends what a great time they had in your company. Well, doing market research for your business is a bit like that. Every person you have dealings with or who comes to buy from you is like a guest at your table. You want them to feel good about doing business with you.

Ask your potential customers the right questions, and they will tell you all you need to know, so that what you supply is right for your market niche – and chances are they will give you lots of other information, too. It doesn't matter how large or small your company is, or how big or little your plans are: you have to get out in the marketplace and get to know every inch of the terrain.

Knowing your competitors and where you stand among them is vital to your business future. Looking at your business through the eyes of the customer, supplier, and competitor is crucial, too. Becoming known and becoming business friends with people who already know the industry is a shortcut to business survival.

> It doesn't matter how large or small your company is, or how big or little your plans are: you have to get out in the marketplace and get to know every inch of the terrain.

Start local

To begin with, your family and friends are likely to be your business territory. Your arena will be very small and very familiar. They are an invaluable starting point because they will be honest with you – if you ask them to be – as my kids were. They used to tell me straight what did and did not work.

When I began my Reggae Reggae Sauce business I spent a lot of time at the local Brixton market, allowing the stallholders time to get familiar with who I was and what I was saying. Your first customers will always be your first customers, and you need to remember to keep them close and treat them well. Loyalty is important. If you keep your early mistakes small-scale and local, you can put them right – quite cheaply – before you start selling further afield.

In some ways your local market will be your fiercest critic as well. I have always said to people, "Tell *me* if something's not right; but if something *is* right, tell everyone else!"

I drew up my first business plan based on how we were doing in the local community, but I didn't have enough understanding about how the food industry worked. I was getting constantly knocked back by the banks and other investors, who weren't convinced by my fledgling business plan. It was time to start looking at the bigger picture and make better decisions about my new business.

I was very lucky because I found a business advisor, Nadia Jones, who understood how the food industry worked. She advised me to start networking at trade shows and exhibitions – to get to know as much as I could about sales, marketing, manufacturing, and promoting sauces, and generally get to know the whole saucy story.

STIRRING UP THE MARKET

Networking is the candy store of business information. The real fun starts here. Get set to start attending exhibitions and trade fairs that specialize in your area of business. These shows are all about selling and making new contacts, so everyone who attends will be keen to show you what they do. You can immerse yourself in a festival of opportunities to find out more about your area of interest and learn about other people's expertise. It's a great way to educate yourself fast in every aspect of what happens in your business.

I learned many new things about the world of sauces. For instance, I found out that there were specialist condiment magazines that write about sauces, so I could contact them for coverage and PR. I learned about new product launches and could see what worked and what didn't. I found out who did what in the sauce business and who was well respected for being good at what they did. I got marketing and merchandising contacts and information from retailers of every size and from all parts of the country. I learned how supermarkets worked, too. So, yes, exhibitions taught me a lot.

Networking is like going into a classroom where everyone is already educated about the subject – but is happy to share what he or she knows. I met so many people who knew more than I did, and, of course, they were looking for information themselves. Everyone wants to know what the latest trends are and to produce the next new thing. So even though I was trying to get a few tips from them, they wanted what I had to offer as well. That's why I say to people that networking is one of the crucial elements of doing business.

> Networking is like going into a classroom where everyone is already educated about the subject – but is happy to share what they know.

At these fabulous events you will meet 'netties' who appear as regular as clockwork. I got to recognize the 'foodie netties' very quickly. They attend all the big shows, such as BBC Good Food Show, the World Food Market, and, if they are setting up in business, the Business Startup Exhibition. I became a 'foodie' because I was always collecting information and business cards, making connections, and being a bit of a busybody, doing anything I could to get myself and the sauce noticed.

I used to go to all kinds of exhibitions. Even at a household exhibition you will find some sort of connection to your product. Any insight that you can get from the people that you're talking to is useful. It may not have value immediately, but in the long term something will come together. Networking is one of the most crucial things you can do in business. It allows you to get alongside those who really know their trade and to get no-holds-barred inside information. Remember, too, that people who are ambitious will change jobs – so the marketing manager you were talking to yesterday could become the group director of a major competitor tomorrow. Friendships grow alongside personal careers, and knowledge grows with them.

Collecting business cards and networking with people in that market niche was all part of the plan. I used to come home every evening with dozens of business cards, and empty out my pockets for the kids to sort out for me. These contacts were my keys to the sauce kingdom, and we would always use them if we needed to find out anything.

Once I opened my mind to how much I had to learn – and quickly – there was no way I was going to miss out on an opportunity to know more. You would find me at any exhibition to do with food. I might be on the trail of information about bottles and bottling, or there would be rules and regulations to learn about or storage techniques to be aware of. I wanted to know about every aspect of the supply chain, from manufacture to how to get a bar code. At that time I assumed that I would need to know how to do everything myself.

LEVI'S TOP TIPS FOR GETTING THE MOST OUT OF TRADE SHOWS AND EXHIBITIONS

- Plan your attack – don't just wander. Show venues are huge, and you need to target your time.
- Plan what you are going to say and the kinds of questions that you want to ask.
- Make sure that you are in a good position in the bar or coffee area at lunchtime.
- If there are specific people you want to meet, get in touch with them at least two months in advance. You will need an appointment.
- Dress to impress, shake hands, and be polite at all times. Wear comfortable shoes!
- Respect people's time. Be friendly, and listen to what they are telling you.
- Don't forget to take your own business cards. Give them out to everyone you meet.
- Sharpen up your business pitch and know your USP.
- When someone gives you their card, make a brief note about them or about the main point discussed. It will help you to remember who they are.
- Follow up with a quick email after the show, so that your details are in your contacts' address books.

UNDERSTANDING YOUR MARKET NICHE

Once you have your idea, you know your USP, and you understand the marketplace, you are in a position to decide where you and your product or service best fit within that market. One of the most common mistakes people make when they are starting out is to try to be all things to all people. That rarely works because potential customers and clients like to be able to understand easily what you are selling, so they can quickly judge whether they want or need your product or service.

Creating a *customer profile* is an important step towards identifying your market niche, and includes important information for your business plan. The name of the brand and its labelling, quality, pricing, and marketing all need to be aimed at the same market and, of course, summed up in your USP.

CREATE A CUSTOMER PROFILE FOR YOUR BUSINESS IDEA

About your market
Ask yourself what niche you are aiming at: mass market, luxury, specialist, professional, consumer, or business?

About your business customers
What is their USP?
What do they want or need from you and your product or service?

What can you offer them?

What do you want or need from them?

Can they provide it?

About your end-customers

Can you visualize what your core customers are like
and what they are looking for?

What are their needs and wants?

How much money do they have to spend?

Will they be more price-conscious or quality-
conscious?

How often will they want to buy what you have
to offer?

Who are your most important customers?

About your competitors

What can you offer that your competitors cannot?

What do they do better than you?

Are their strengths a threat to your plans, or are you
creating a different niche?

What do you need to do to stand out from your
competitors?

Does your USP reflect where you are headed?

About your vision

Where do you see yourself and your company...

... in the short term (1–2 years)?

... in the medium term (3–5 years)?

... in the long term (5 years +)?

Market classification

The consumer market is made up of the kinds of goods and services that you will see on the High Street or find easily online. Consumer goods are price-sensitive and often mass market. The volume of sales can vary from month to month according to the season, and the popularity of the brand may depend on trends.

Other goods and services are sold 'business to business' and are highly specialist. In the food industry, that applies to the companies who manufacture the sauce bottles and packaging materials, for example. They sell, in bulk, to food and drink producers. The price per unit may be very low, but they are selling in huge volume to make their profits.

All of the products produced by the Levi Roots Reggae Reggae companies are mass-market consumer products. We buy the raw products from industry specialists, but we are selling to consumers (via the retailers). The labelling shouts Caribbean sunshine, fun times, and good flavour; the pricing tells you that we are aiming at the average household. It is really important that our supply keeps up with the pace of consumer demand. We have to keep our message consistent, too.

Every business sector is divided into market niches. Classification is everything. Retailers, especially, like to classify products so that they know where to put them on the shelf, and so that they can keep track of who is buying them. The music industry, for example, is divided into sectors such as pop, classical, jazz, world music, blues, reggae, R&B.

The underground

Then there will be a 'niche within a niche', which is more specialized – it's what people call the 'underground'. It is often the underground market niche that sets the trend and determines what is ready to become mainstream. The investors, the trendsetters, and the grass-roots people will be the ones who discover new talent and original businesses first.

> It is often the underground market niche that sets the trend and determines what is ready to become mainstream.

Richard Branson is an example of an entrepreneur who understands the appeal of niche branding very well. He's a leading international businessman who has mainstream respect, but he is still loved by underground people because he has stayed true to his independent and trailblazing roots.

Roots Reggae Reggae Sauce Ltd launched in a niche market. When I first started out, my market was mainly the Caribbean community – and I was proud and happy with that. Reggae Reggae Sauce was stocked only in the Caribbean sections of small London supermarkets and in a few localized areas. But one of my ambitions is to make Caribbean food as universally popular as Indian, Thai, or Chinese food. To achieve that, I am working with Peter Jones and the team to broaden the appeal of the Levi Roots range way beyond the niche of Caribbean food and to create a brand that is mainstream. Reggae Reggae Sauce is now a staple item in every supermarket in the UK. So the niche within the niche has grown and is now becoming bigger than the original niche itself! (There is more about our business strategy and how to achieve this in Chapter 5.)

Everything associated with the Levi Roots brand is a way of leading people towards an awareness of Caribbean music and culture, and the fabulocious taste of Caribbean food. We want to keep our niche identity while still being instantly recognizable in the mainstream market. But it is still important to stay true to our underground roots. If your original customers think that you have abandoned your roots, they will stop trusting the brand, and you will lose your credibility and your place in the market very quickly.

> If your original customers think you have abandoned your roots, you will lose your credibility and your place in the market very quickly.

This also happens in industries other than the food industry. For example, when the reggae band Aswad hit the mainstream music charts in the 1990s, they introduced a whole new section of people to reggae music. Aswad stayed true to their niche market and remained a pure reggae band. But through their phenomenal popular success they helped to make the pop reggae niche larger than the roots reggae music sector they came from – and made it easier for others who followed them.

THE CHUTNEY EXAMPLE

Chutneys are popular and are found in most kitchens, but the chutney niche itself has many niches.

- Chutney A is a mass-market brand that sells in high volume at a low price. What you see is what you get. Everybody buys it. It is on the weekly shopping list. It has few competitors apart from supermarket own brands. Market share: 80 per cent.

- Chutney B is a mid-range brand that specializes in mass-produced 'home-made' chutneys. It has a higher price point than Chutney A, but sells in lower volume. It is an occasional purchase for some and a regular purchase for others who have a higher food budget. Customers may buy Chutney A *and* Chutney B. Market share: 15 per cent.

- Chutney C is a newcomer to the market. It is a brand of 'home-made' chutney that is also *organic*. It is not mass-produced and so it cannot keep up with the mass turnover of a supermarket chain. It is a potential competitor for Chutney B in the long term, but in the short term it is available in more specialist outlets and delicatessens. It is seen as a luxury and health product. The product is high-priced, but sells in low volume. Chutney C customers may never buy Chutney A. Market share: 5 per cent.

Each of these chutneys is also in a niche of its own: mass market, home-made, or organic. It's good to go for a market niche because, if you forge a place within it, you can become a leader in that market.

DON'T COMPARE YOURSELF WITH OTHERS

Back in the 1970s, I had a band called Matic16. I couldn't get a record deal at the time, but I knew that we were producing a good roots reggae sound and I understood the market niche, so I decided to do things my way.

I set up the Conqueror (UK) record label in 1981 as a way of launching my own music and keeping control of the profits – and so that I wouldn't have to rely on others. The music industry operated on a sale-or-return basis at that time, and the average discount was 50 per cent. If we pressed 100 singles (all in vinyl in those days), I knew that all the profit would come back to the label – but only if all the copies sold.

As the music started to make money, we ploughed the profits straight back into the business and began to invest in other young talent as well. My love for reggae music meant that I truly understood the market. When I heard a good reggae sound, I knew exactly how good it was and whether or not we could sell that track. I wanted the label to draw more attention to reggae music and widen its appeal. An early single, 'Jahovia', was a great hit and is still an iconic roots and culture track today; there were plenty of others as well. Ricky Ranking was one of our earliest finds. He cut his first album with Endeavour Records and is still going strong today as a member of Roots Manuva.

But Conqueror wasn't only about making money; we wanted the artists to understand how to protect their interests, too. We used to walk them down to the PRS

(Performing Rights Society) and encourage them to sign up, so that their future rights and interests were protected.

There were ten of us in the band and, although the label was set up with my money, we all shared the work. I was the lead singer and also helped the bands to write songs. Patrick Tenyue, the horn player, trained and found new talent. His brother, Henry 'Buttons' Tenyue, played trombone and also booked the studio space and handled production. Our drummer was Barrington, then we had Philip, the percussionist; Samson, our guitarist; Paul, the keyboard player; James, who played bass; Vivian, the keyboard player; and Flutie, the flute player.

We would run off between 100 and 500 records at a time and deliver them personally to record stores around the UK. We would 'sell them in' in tens and twenties, and then phone up the stockists regularly to see how things were going. Sometimes we would even send our own customers down to a particular store to help boost those early sales – which would encourage the DJs to give the track more air time.

Getting to know the DJs personally over many months meant that they came to trust our music and were more likely to take a new release. We took our music to the pirate radio stations – and may have used the old 'payola' on a few occasions to get more air time (meaning that we slipped the DJ a couple of pounds to play our music). These days it would be called a marketing campaign, and there is a corporate version of payola in the form of fees and rates for play time. Back then it was all about personal relationships within the industry – and a shared love of the music.

We kept an eye on sales and would keep the stock topped up as necessary. We paid attention to areas where the singles weren't selling, and we would act fast to put things right. For example, if sales of a new release were strong in our local area of Brixton, but poor in the borough of Hammersmith, we would get down there and play a few gigs to increase our following. Those were fun days – and we learned a lot about business while we closed those early deals. They were lessons that would be valuable to me in my later business ventures and dealings.

Yes, we took risks, but they were calculated risks because we understood the music – our product – and we knew our market. We wanted to prepare more people to understand the risks involved within the industry.

The band broke up only when the Tenyue brothers were head-hunted by a new reggae band on the popular music circuit called UB40. (If you can remember the early 1980s, then you will know their music well.) That in itself was an important business lesson for me. Because you must always allow people on your team to fulfil their potential, talented people often leave a thriving business. The answer is always to be prepared for contingencies – and always have a plan B. My plan B was to return to my solo career, which I did, and which I am still enjoying (when time allows). When I perform some of Matic16's lead singles these days, people are astonished to discover that the voice is Levi Roots. In those days I was still Keith Graham, and there were a lot of business lessons still to come.

THE LEARNING NEVER STOPS

I've always believed that I can do anything I set my mind
to – provided there is a basic level of ability there to begin
with. At the end of the day it is all about setting your own
pace and working hard to achieve what you want. Make
sure that you are never your own problem, by getting all the
information you need to be prepared. You can never know
too much. For example, for a while, in the early 90s, I cut off
my dreadlocks and became a mortgage advisor. I can't
imagine myself doing that now, but it was the Thatcher era
and the time of the 'yuppies' (young urban professionals).
I was young and anything seemed possible. I never had
any training for anything like that, but I just found myself in a
position where I applied for a job. I had to study for endless
exams to qualify, and I made it. I believed I could do it if I
was positive enough about achieving the end result. I knew
that I wasn't my problem, and that is still my philosophy.

Be true to yourself and be honest with yourself, and
you will get the *best* from yourself. Sourcing the information
you need is all about education. It is never too late to learn,
and it is important to discover how broad your skills are and
to make the most of them.

During my music career, I hadn't needed to use a
computer, but once I had decided to focus on selling my
sauce, I knew I had to learn if I were to be taken seriously
in the business world. I was in my forties when I took myself
back to my local Brixton College to do an IT course. I also
joined basic graphic design classes, just so that I could
create my own sauce labels and save money on paying

a designer. When you don't have the money to pay other people to do things, you really have to rely upon your dormant skills. But I enjoyed it. It felt personal and made me feel part of the whole process of creating my product.

In the early days, it is worth trying to do some things yourself – setting up a website, organizing mailings, creating leaflets, and so on – provided you get some training first. You will learn more about your abilities and you will also be in a better position to brief someone else to do those things for you, once the business is off the ground.

> **There are two things that are always better done by experts: one is your accounts and the other is your legal agreements. Some things cannot be learned in enough depth at evening classes.**

Don't stand in your own way

We all have dormant skills within us – it's a question of whether we choose to raise them up and use them, and how passionate we are about learning new things. I really wanted to learn, and so I knew it was in me to do so. I think everybody has that capacity. If you really need to do something, you will usually be able to learn how to do it, if only for the short time that the skill is useful.

Sometimes, however, we need encouragement to get started, and that is where getting professional advice can be invaluable. There is more support available for start-up companies today than ever before, and you will speed yourself on your business journey much more quickly if you seek out some help and advice. My journey took me to an organization called Greater London Enterprise, and to an advisor called Nadia Jones, who eventually helped me to secure £1,000 to pay for the labels that went on the bottles everyone saw on *Dragons' Den*.

PUT YOURSELF IN A POSITIVE STATE OF MIND

Most people who are thinking of changing direction will try to find a new job while they are still employed, and that is a wise way to approach setting up a business, too. If you start by running your own show alongside the day job, you can test the water and get a lot of things in place before you go solo.

Running your own business may be your ultimate goal, but you need to be ready, and to be sure it is going to work, before your jeopardize your livelihood – especially when you have seven children to buy new trainers for, as I did. A thing like asking your bank manager for a business loan is totally different to asking for a top-up loan to do up your kitchen or buy a refrigerator. It is a new approach completely. But there comes a time when you are ready to take off your working coat and put on your own logo.

> You need to change your mind-set and begin to think differently.

The moment you decide to run your own show, everything changes. From that point on, you will be taking control of every aspect of your business and managing your own time.

Part of starting up in business involves getting yourself ready. The first step is to put yourself into a business owner's mind-set and begin to think differently. Start to look, dress, and talk the part as well. Walk the talk, get to know people who can help you, and start asking them the right questions.

It is now all about how you are going to make things happen – rather than reacting to what other people want you to do. Now other people are reacting to what *you* are doing. The next stage in the process is to find a mentor, and hopefully he or she will guide you towards the other tools you will need.

If you find yourself faltering on your path, it is always worth revisiting your dream of yourself as a success, just to get an extra boost of self-belief. Nothing can stop you from making a success of your plans – except the power of your mind. I have always said to myself, "It may not happen overnight; I may need to work a little harder than all the other guys, but there is no reason why I can't make it."

At the time I made the decision to leave my job at Plumbase, in February 2006, I had reached the moment when I wanted to control my own destiny.

PROVIDING THE RIGHT SUPPORT TO MAKE THINGS HAPPEN

Nadia Jones has been a business advisor and mentor for more than 15 years, mainly working with young disadvantaged and long-term unemployed clients to help them develop business ideas, write business plans, attract funding, and establish viable sustainable businesses. I first met her when she was a business advisor for creative industries with GLE oneLondon in Brixton, south London. Before that she worked for the Prince's Trust helping to establish their business programme for the 18–30 age group.

Starting a business can be quite a challenge, particularly if you have no experience of the business world or do not know anyone who is an entrepreneur or successfully self-employed. Many people can be overawed by having to go to see somebody who's suited and booted, especially someone such as a bank manager. They may feel that they are not going to be listened to, and sometimes they are right. That's when consulting a business advisor or finding a suitable business mentor to advise you can be particularly useful – to ensure that you are fully prepared and have all the right skills and business understanding that you need in order to succeed.

Nadia Jones, business advisor

"I first met Levi when I was working in Lambeth for Greater London Enterprise (GLE1 as it was known). I knew the community and, because of my past experience, I felt there might be people in that area who were not getting the intensive support they required to get their businesses off the ground. My role was to help people to understand how to raise finance and build up their soft skills like confidence and communication skills.

Levi's personal journey is inspirational for others. From our first meeting in August 2006 to the moment he appeared on *Dragons' Den* was only six months! It's quite amazing what can happen when someone's passion is coupled with hard work and self-discipline, and the determination to step outside their comfort zone.

That, for me as a business advisor, is what it's all about. That's why I have spent so much time working with those who other people might term 'disadvantaged'. I've worked with young people, ex-offenders, a lot of lone parents, and those from ethnic minorities. It's amazing because they are often among the most entrepreneurial. All they need is the right support or the right word at the right time.

A lot of people who come to see me have already tried the conventional routes, and they are often quite downcast. It's particularly rewarding to work with people who go on to make a successful business when they've previously been turned away.

I am passionate about the work that I do, and I like to be able to draw out the same passion in others. Levi is so right in what he says. Once people connect with their passion and start to believe it and live it, then that can really take them a long way.

Not everyone who comes to see me will ultimately start a business. Sometimes it takes a while for the individual to realize that, but the most important thing is that they will have gained valuable skills that can help them in other areas of life.

HOW A BUSINESS ADVISOR WORKS

A business advisor needs to be a good listener. I want to find out as much as I can about what's brought someone to the point where they are sitting in front of me saying, 'I want to do this more than anything.'

Most people working as business advisors will begin by asking a series of basic questions such as the following:

- Have you had any previous business experience?
- Have you done any test trading, no matter how limited?
- Do you have any finance to put towards your business?
- What scale have you worked on previously? (For example, if you are in catering, what is the largest event you have catered for?)
- Have you tried to make a prototype of your product or trialled your service?

The answers give a sense of the person's potential. It's always interesting to see what someone has done under their own steam. I look at their drive and their determination to make their business work and get it off the ground.

I get many people to work far harder than I think they have ever worked in the past, and I try to really get them thinking, as well as building them up as people. It's not just about building a business; it's about building the person, too. A business person needs to have confidence.

No one said it would be easy

I tell people that there is much more to running a business than being good at what they do. I am there to facilitate their plans, but also to let them know that working for themselves can be difficult – because of the many different things that they will have to do themselves.

If you are setting up on your own, *you* will be the person who does everything in the early stages: you will be your PR person, your marketeer; you will be networking; you will be the one keeping track of your spending and trying to keep on top of your finances.

There are many new things that as a start-up entrepreneur you need to be willing to attempt – to a level that enables you to go into the market *at least* at the level of your competitors. Because if you are not going to go in at the level of your competitors, there is no point in starting up.

NADIA'S ADVICE FOR BUSINESS START-UPS

Action planning

No matter how basic, creating an action plan is very important.

Market research

Who are your competitors? If you can think of only one, then you have not done your research properly. What information can you find out? What is their pricing structure? What can you find out that is beneficial to you?

Find your point of difference

What makes you think that you have a greater USP than your main competitor? You want to expand the market – but not necessarily jump into the same market. I talk a lot about market saturation. There is a good time to get started in a market and a not-so-good time, so that's part of the research and the homework you would have to do.

Financial planning

Under-capitalization and badly managed cash flow are the two main reasons for business failure. Financial planning is very important. If you have very high overheads, it's going to impact on a potential business. If you need several thousand pounds per month to live on, now may not be the time to start that business. Ask yourself:

- What are your personal expenses? How much do you need, realistically, to keep your household ticking over, particularly if you have dependants?
- What have you allowed as working capital?
- What money do you need for equipment?
- What will your business need to turn over on a weekly basis? On a monthly basis? Will this cover your expenses or other people's wages, too?

Be realistic

People's sales expectations are usually far too high, and their estimates of personal expenses too low. Unfortunately, costs are ever-increasing, so it is important to be realistic about this at the planning stage.

Most people underestimate their costs. They may say, 'I want to run a restaurant, and I want to do it on £25,000,' when in reality the running costs may be nearer £125,000. Ask yourself what makes you think that you can run a restaurant if you've never run one before, with all that this entails.

Go and look at your competitors. Find out how a chef you admire got started. It doesn't necessarily have to be someone in your locality. Read the biographies of established restaurateurs. Make sure that you get your planning and your figures accurate.

Forward planning

What are you going to do if your sales are not as good as you had forecast? Have you got a plan B, C, or even D? Often the answer is no. An advisor will help you to construct a contingency plan and explain why it might be wiser to build up your business alongside your other jobs. This kind of approach has really helped people over the first year or two.

Priorities

The first priority is putting together a business plan. A lot of people begin by wanting to spend money instead of making it. For example, they may say, "I would love to have premises." If that sounds like you, ask yourself:

- What could you do in premises that you don't feel you could do at home, on a market stall, or in somebody else's stall or shop?
- Why is it that you feel you will be more successful opening up premises of your own, if you've never done anything like that before and if you don't yet know the going rate in the area for rent?

Discipline

You need to be self-disciplined to be a success in business, especially when controlling your cash flow. Whether you are happier keeping track of your costs on paper or on computer, you need to be disciplined about updating your expenditure – probably on a daily basis.

As a start-up entrepreneur, you will need to take on skills and a mind-set that may feel alien to you or that you have not been able to achieve in the past. If the business is to work, and to start working from day one, you need to develop a high degree of self-discipline.

This isn't just about stocking your shop or getting the right products for your customers – it also involves looking regularly at the sales and expenses. This means keeping a close eye on money coming in relative to money going out. A business support advisor can help you find a way to keep on top of finances.

CONFIDENCE BUILDING

Not everyone recognizes their own achievements or skills. A would-be caterer may say that they have only catered for three events – but if there were 40 people at each event, that's 120 people! In that case, they've already done quite a bit, and this is something we can build on. It's about instilling confidence and focus – based on reality, not speculation.

Communication skills

I try to help the individuals I work with to understand that the way in which they communicate can really improve their confidence. If you find it hard to make yourself understood or are worried about using the right words, then that is something that can easily be worked on.

Networking

Levi talks a lot about networking and it is something he does very naturally. I am passionate about networking – because I know it works and I have seen it in action. But not everyone welcomes the idea.

The trick is to prepare in advance. Have a few relevant sentences planned, so that you introduce yourself effectively. Pluck up courage and speak to somebody, or let someone come and speak to you. Listen well: you want to find out as much as you can about that person. They may not be a potential customer – but they may know someone who could be. Focus on someone else rather than yourself and it will be much easier than you expect."

Think outside the box

Your mind is powerful, so even if you are restricted by money, time, or other considerations, when you want something badly enough you have the capacity to achieve it. I work with people to help them think creatively. A good business advisor will work with you to help you put the practical steps in place to get you to where you want to go.

The likeability factor

It may be a cliché, but it is still true: people buy people. If your likeability factor is high up the scale and you learn to be good at communicating, you will be able to talk about your idea and make progress much more quickly.

Levi has great personal presence – there is no doubt about it. I had a very good feeling about Levi when I first met him, and I just hoped that when he started to talk about his business idea I wouldn't be disappointed. But I needn't have worried. The degree of preparation that Levi had already gone into before he came to see me was impressive, and he was also grounded and realistic about how he wanted to approach starting his business.

Levi would have made a success of his business even if *Dragons' Den* had not come along – but he has shown how to make the most of opportunities and has fast developed into a respected businessman in his own right. Perhaps his greatest skills are his desire to keep learning, his ability to listen, and his awareness of when to ask for advice."

CHAPTER 3

WHAT'S IN A PLAN?

Roots of success 3:
The plan is your key to success

*"Life is one big road with lots of signs.
So when you riding through the ruts, don't
complicate your mind."*

BOB MARLEY

Bob Marley knew a thing or two about staying focused on the road you have chosen without getting distracted along the way. But to do that you need to know where you are heading, and to get there you need a plan.

Most successful entrepreneurs are people of action. They like to make decisions quickly and to see results. When you are raring to get started with a new business, it can be hard to sit down and focus on planning. But it is important not to try to run before you have learned to walk. Only *you* know what you are trying to achieve; only *you* know what your dream of success holds. Writing it down will force you to look deep inside yourself and help you to recognize what the real you is all about.

> Do not attempt to get away with not doing a watertight business plan, and make sure that you do it yourself – only you know what is best.

A plan is important for many reasons. It is your road map and your recipe for success rolled into one. Preparing it will focus your mind on your vision and your USP. It is also an important document to show to other people, especially investors. If you delay creating a plan, then you delay taking control of your venture. The danger is that decisions are then made in an ad hoc way as you drift along. Before you know it, you have lost sight of the big picture, and you are simply reacting to whatever happens next.

Make the most of this planning time and take it seriously. Your plan will keep you on track when you are up to your ears in business. It will stop you having to start from scratch with every new decision – because you will look at the plan and say, "Ah, yes, we're on track" or "No, this isn't what I'm about". When you hit a few ruts, you won't get thrown off the road because you will still have the bigger picture in mind.

I had no idea how to put together a business plan when I first started, so I looked for guidance on the internet. You will find help everywhere once you start to look. The Further Resources on page 275 will give you some places to start.

CHOOSING YOUR BUSINESS INGREDIENTS

To cook up a successful business, you need to choose quality ingredients. But first you need to decide who you are cooking for and how many are coming to dinner, so that you can set your budget and plan the menu. Only then will you know which ingredients you need.

What kind of business are you dreaming of making a success? Where do you see your business, and yourself, in six months, one year, three years, or five years? Is it a product or a service? How much do you know about the field you are going into? Do you know the difference between a limited company and being a sole trader? Do you understand a balance sheet? Have you learned the difference between gross profit and net profit? What skills do you have to make your business work? And who do you know who has the rest of the skills you need? Many people starting up a new business will have some commercial experience, but a surprising number have none at all.

The planning stage is a step to take seriously. Fans of *Dragons' Den* will know that the vast majority of people whose business pitches fail apart have not prepared all their business ingredients. Something is missing. Prepare your business plan as if *you* were appearing on *Dragons' Den*. In fact, you will be doing something similar every time you pitch to a new customer, every time you try to sell your products, every time you speak to the bank manager about investment.

PUTTING EVERYTHING IN THE MIX

Your business plan has to be as much about you as about your business, reflecting your preparation and your enthusiasm for the long-term vision. All the knowledge you acquired during your market research will now be turned to practical advantage. Everything you know must now come out in the business plan, direct from you.

> Your plan has to be as much about you as about your business, reflecting your preparation and your enthusiasm for the long-term vision.

ONE STEP AT A TIME

Your plan will take time to do properly. Don't expect to be able to prepare it all at the last minute before your presentation to the bank. It has to be like the foundations of a house: well constructed, it is built to last.

However, keep it clear and simple. This is not a piece of creative writing – it is a set of plans and directions showing how you plan to make more money than you spend. Don't complicate things by including good intentions and imaginings. Here are the main elements it should contain:

Your objective

This is a short statement of why you have created your business plan and the period it covers. Include a short contents list with page numbers, so that investors can navigate it easily. Some people will only look at this first page, so make it sharp.

The business opportunity

Your plan needs an overview of why there is a gap in the market and how you will fill it. This is your supporting evidence. It tells potential investors that you have done your homework and that there is a genuine opportunity out there.

Unique Selling Point (USP)

What you have to offer is different. Your USP is a statement of why it (the product or service) will work and why consumers and clients will want to buy it. This is a vital point, and I talk about it some more on page 37.

Sales and marketing strategy

What are your ideas for reaching your target market? This section tells people how, why, and when are you planning to roll out your plan. How much will it cost per month? What could you do for free? Go back to that SWOT analysis you did (see page 46) and include that, too. Show everyone that you are aware of the threats to your business idea and how you plan to turn them into a winning opportunity.

Sales forecast and costings

Break down the number of units you expect to sell on a month-by-month basis (or how many projects you expect to sign), and specify how much money you expect to come in and when. A well-constructed sales model (for example on a computer spreadsheet) will enable you to 'test' different projected levels of sales and work out the likely effect on your cash flow and profitability. All the numbers must add up. Be careful not to overestimate this figure. Entrepreneurs are optimists and think that everyone else will love their product just as much as they do. Always make a prototype, test a sample, or try selling locally or on a small scale first.

Business operations

How are you going to source, manufacture, quality-check, and deliver your product to your marketplace? Where will you store your goods? What will the costs be?

The team

Who do you have on board to help you deliver your plan, what will each person be doing, and what experience do they have? (This includes your associates such as your accountant or business mentor.) How much will they cost?

Annual budget

This ties in with your sales forecast and includes a summary of your spending and your revenues, month by month, across every area of the company.

Investment

The investment you are looking for and the period of time over which you need it. What will be the return on that investment (the profit) if you manage to do as well as your sales forecast suggests?

The vision

Why you? What motivates you? What are your skills? What makes you qualified to secure and protect the investment? If you have a business CV (resumé), this is where you should include it, focused towards your business sector.

Your driving ambition remains as important as ever – but in your business plan try not to show too much emotional attachment to your product or idea. Investors, should you need them, may not like that. They will want to see your passion directed towards being in business for profit and growth, which at some point will involve making some tough decisions. Too much attachment to the idea for its own sake can be sentimental and irrational. That can be dangerous for your financial wellbeing and business security.

> Passion is the driver, but in your plan try not to be too emotionally attached to your product or idea. Investors, should you need them, may not like that. They will want to see a flair for being in business for profit and growth, which will involve making some tough decisions.

PLANNING IS FOR THE LONG TERM

Instant returns are a myth, won only occasionally on the lottery. In business, you need to act swiftly to make things happen, but the results may come slowly, so planning for the long term is important. It will help you to dream bigger dreams, make more ambitious plans, and remain patient when the results don't appear instantly. It's about knowing that success will not come overnight, but that it *will* come. You will work for it, but you will deserve it – and it will be worth waiting for.

Many people new to business will have to learn adjust their expectations of how quickly things will happen and break down their long-term plan into smaller goals. As in any race, the first part is always the hardest: deciding when and where you'll make your move in order to get ahead of your competitors. But it is important to know what stage you are at on the track, recognize how long each stage will take, and to understand how valuable the outcome will be.

A business needs time to grow and mature, to make its mark within its niche. The longer you nurture the growth of your business and the stronger it becomes, the more profit you will make. So it is crucial to see the bigger picture. Learning to recognize the right moment to expand, merge, or sell comes later, and that will need a plan, too.

> Profit equals time. It's about knowing that success will not come overnight, but it will come. You will work for it, but you will deserve it – and it will be worth waiting for.

WHAT'S THE COST?

With your in-depth knowledge of the marketplace, awareness of your competitors, self-confidence, newly learned business skills, and all those hundreds of contacts you made at festivals and business events, you can begin to assess the profitability of your concept. And the first place to start is with the topic of costings.

You need to figure out answers to the following:
• What's it going to cost you to set up your business?
• How much will each item cost to produce?
• How many units and at what price do you need to sell at to break even?

- What is your profit likely to be for any given level of sales?
- How much funding do you need?
- Where's the investment money going to come from?
- Are you being realistic with your plans?
- Is it a profitable idea?

But to start with, you need to make a very long list of costs, to include every item at every stage of the process from the beginning to the end.

Costing Reggae Reggae Sauce

When costing my sauce, I thought about one batch of sauce (64 bottles) at a time. It was quite simple in those days. I worked out how much each of the following stages would cost per batch:
- Buy the ingredients
- Buy the bottles
- Make the labels
- Cook the sauce
- Store the sauce
- Travel to sell the sauce

Adding all the above totals together, I had the cost of one batch of 64 bottles, so I could then work out the amount per unit. In addition, I had to know the following:
- Who was I going to sell it to?
- How many units would they buy?
- How long would it take me to sell all the bottles?

I also had to work out how long this would take me so I could put in a realistic cost for my own time. There's no point working 15 hours a day if your profit works out at only a few pounds per hour. Knowing the above helped me to work out what price I would need to sell it for to make a profit. See page 229 for a definition of profit-and-loss that will help you to work this out yourself.

When I started I was relying on my family as a cheap (or free!) workforce. I had no overheads to pay because it all happened in my kitchen at home. We were learning as we went along, as many start-up businesses do.

These days it is a bit more complicated, and the costings are prepared by our suppliers and the finance team. But the buck still stops with me, and I need to understand those figures, without any doubt. Learning on a small scale is so valuable. You will then be able to apply the lessons that you have learned every step of the way as you grow. The principles are just the same when you are selling millions of units – it's just that everything is on a larger scale.

GET READY TO GET STARTED

Developing the habit of planning and preparing before you take action is vital to your future success – at every stage of your business development. Once you have started on your journey, you will be relying on the thoroughness and accuracy of your early research and development. It will hold you up if you have to go back and start again. Once you are ready, give yourself time to pause and focus: to bring your vision into the present. At this point I suggest a little nap. Just to revisit that dream: you know, the one where the plan works out perfectly. Ahh – sweet dreams!

LEVI'S ORIGINAL BUSINESS PLAN

Here is the original business plan that I created for Reggae Reggae Sauce. As you can see, it wasn't a full business plan with the detailed capital requirements, projected profit and loss models and cash flow projections that a bank or other investor would normally expect to see. In spite of the Dragons not approving of the finances, the plan covers the basic ground necessary to make an impact on investors. While I was putting my plan together, I thought of it as a great big recipe, which would contain all the ingredients necessary for cooking up a delicious result.

Business Plan for REGGAE REGGAE SAUCE

Presented by **Levi Roots**

Business plan date
Thursday, 7th November 2006

Contents

1. EXECUTIVE SUMMARY

Business concept
The products and services:
1. Barbecue/Jerk Sauce
2. Seasoning, Marinade
3. Catering

Projection:

Year	£ turnover
2007–2008	200,000
2008–2009	350,000
2009–2010	1m

Source of start-up funds:

Family	3,000
GLE oneLondon	1,000
Other	2,000
Funds needed	50,000

Application of funds:
• Expansion
• Promotion

2. BUSINESS BACKGROUND

2.1 Projected Business Activity

• The aim of the business is to manufacture and promote our products of hot spicy barbecue sauce and seasonings as essential household food item for lovers of spicy foods/also to add to the ever-growing West Indian jerk/bbq sauce/condiment market our unique tried-and-tested family recipes.

• To exploit to the full the marketing ability of our brand name and logos, not only here in the UK but also Europe and USA via the Press, Radio, TV and other national and international media.

• Reggae Reggae Sauce is already making a name for itself: it is the first condiment food item to be available in record shops.

• Very popular among young people as a spicy full-of-flavour alternative to normal ketchup.

2.2 Legal Business Description: Sole trader

The business Reggae Reggae Sauce is wholly owned by Keith Graham (Levi Roots). There are interested potential partners and careful consideration is being taken about partnership/limited company.

2.3 Financial Projections

Year	Projected
2007–2008	200,000 units
2008–2009	350,000 units
2009–2010	500,000 units

2.4 Owner's Experience

35 years in marketing and promotion as singer/songwriter/record label owner and chef Levi Roots. Nominated for a Mobo Award 1998, toured Europe, Asia, and USA. 15 years' experience as Carnival chef. Creator of Reggae Reggae Sauce business and recipes.

2.5 Support Team

1. Anita Flowers. Marketing manager (MA Creative writing BA Hons Communication)
2. Jeffery Simon. Chef/Caterer
3. Seymour Bowen. Chef/Driver

2.6 Future Staff Requirements

Driver
Chefs: 1–2
Worker
Total: 4–5

2.7 External Support

Nadia Jones (GLE oneLondon)
Bernice D Graham (Financial Adviser)
Jeffery Simon (Chef)
Sharlene Williams

2.8 Employment Policies

In all matters relating to future staff employment, Reggae Reggae Sauce will give utmost consideration to the preservation of good staff relations, training, developments and employment opportunities.

3. AIMS AND OBJECTIVES

3.1 Mission Statement
I would like to make our sauces the first 'Superstar Sauces'. With the marketing ability of the name Reggae Reggae Sauce and my ties and links with the entertainment industry the mission is to make this jerk/barbecue sauce trendy and appealing and affordable to consumers both young and old.

3.2 Business Objectives
• To seek to lower cost, ie: ingredients, bottles, labels
• To raise awareness by promotion
• Secure distribution arrangements
Key objective
• 'Sachet o' sauce'
• Making our sauce more accessible to potential customers
• Marketing my Sachet Box creation
• Still the same great taste and flavours of Reggae Reggae Sauce, but available in sachets all neatly packed in a fashionable box of twelve (12)

4. PRODUCTS AND SERVICES

4.1 Products and Services
• Hot, mild and Smokey sauces
• Made to an age-old Caribbean recipe. Can be use as a marinade, dip, garnish, or flavouring. Made principally from Scotch Bonnet peppers, scallion, garlic, herbs and spices the blend has been described as "The Tastiest Jerk/BBQ Sauce in the World"
• Prompt deliveries
• Jerk seasoning (Will be introduced soon)
• All-purpose seasonings (dry)
• Catering: THE RASTA'RANT SHOW
• Culinary Arts Performance

4.2 Competitive Advantages
The product has been fifteen (15) years in the making.

People trust the taste knowing it is made to home-made traditions. The advantage of marketing is in the name and logos of the product not only here in the UK but also on an international stage.

4.3 Technology and Processes
Bottling and labelling machines are the two greatest needs for the company. They will enable us to produce much faster, more efficient and safer business.
The usage of a computer/electronic cash register and telephones will also be vital.

4.4 Customer Service
The company aims to provide a top class service to our customers and seek to improve the level of service as our company grows with the help of their business. The utmost care will be taken with all matters concerning production and packaging and dealing with customer relations.

5. THE MARKET
5.1 Industry Overview
The exotic spice and sauce market is an ever-expanding industry. It offers great opportunities for investments as more and more people look to the food industry as a means to make money. Also the increasing diversity of the UK allows people to be more exposed to newer foods and exotic recipes. Tesco's now stock a huge range of Afro-Caribbean sauces, spices, seasoning and other condiments from around the world that used to only be available on local market stalls.

5.2 Customer Profile
Our typical customer:
• Likes hot food
• Doesn't mind it spicy
• Vegetarians
• Fast-food diners (chicken shop etc)
• Restaurants
• Take aways
• Barbecues/parties

5.3 Competition

1. Walkers Wood: Jamaican jerk/bbq sauces, seasonings and marinades distributed by Tesco stores.
2. Encona: hot/mild jerk pepper sauce. Widely available
3. Grace Jerk sauce and seasoning

5.4 External Influences

GLE oneLondon is a business advice service based in south London. They have been of great help with advice and some financial help to the business, and I continue to liaise with Nadia Jones and Sunita Bhwane.

5.5 Environmental Issues

We care for the planet, that is why we will seek to include an environmental policy as part of our business plans.
We will look at containers, packaging and fuel with intention to eventually go green in our entire production of Reggae Reggae Sauce.

6. MARKETING

6.1 Message

REGGAE REGGAE SAUCE: Put music in your food
THE TASTIEST JERK/BBQ SAUCE IN THE WORLD

6.2 Positioning

I want our competitors to view our products and company's strategy as working to a very high standard with quality goods.
The reputation of the company's name, logos, and preserving the taste and flavours will be of paramount interest to us as a business.

6.3 Branding

We will exploit the company's logos and branding to the full. With my experience in the entertainment world, having friends and associates in the Reggae industry here in the UK, Jamaica and America, and being an international reggae music artist myself, we think there are open opportunities to be exploited.

6.4 Pricing Objectives

Our pricing objective is to maintain our high standard of production, to keep manufacturing cost down while increasing the company's profit margin. This will allow us to share our benefits with customers and consumers through lower prices, savings, and faster production output.

6.5 Price Determination

Cost: 0.32p per bottle

Distribution price:	0.90p
Wholesale price:	1.25p
RRP:	1.49p
Profit:	138%

6.6 Price Adjustment Strategies

Purchasing bottles, labels, ingredients and packaging in advance (savings)
Bulk buying (savings)
The introduction of other products, ie seasonings and recipes (possible increase/savings)
Packaging adjustments (possible increase)
Adding different flavors to the taste range (possible increase)

6.7 Marketing Methods

We will market the business through the music and entertainment industry. Initially, mass advertising campaign on the local pirate radio stations, sponsorships, and interviews on TV, press, and leafleting.

7. SALES

7.1 Sales Channels
- Distribution (wholesale)
- Deliveries (direct)
- Online (sales and transactions)
- Catering (festivals, carnivals, fairs etc)
- Other

7.2 Sales Personnel
Anita Flowers, Marketing manager. MA Creative Writing; BA (Hons) Communication.

7.3 Lead Processing
- Enquiries will be handled professionally.
- All customer information updated and easily accessible.

7.4 Invoicing and Payment Collection
All invoicing will be direct. Customer will be prompted to make payments due on time by:
- Barclay's business account
- Online banking
- Cash. Cheques

8. FINANCE

8.1 Investment Needed
50,000 pounds

8.2 Application of Funds
This money will be used to finance acquisition of the following:

Premises/rent/rates	10,000
Shop fitting	10,000
Bottles + tops (pallets)	5,000
Closures	2,000
Labels designs	2,000
Transport/insurance	4,500
Logos/promotion	2,500
Ingredients	2,500
Office equipment (computers/tills etc)	2,500
Total	41,000

8.3 Assumptions
1. All future forecast figures are based on sales from August–October 2006.
2. Assumptions on growth are based on sales for London only.
3. Other

CHAPTER 4

STARTING UP

Roots of success 4:
Find yourself a mentor

> *"There is always more than one path to follow to get to your destination."*

LEVI ROOTS

First-time entrepreneurs, especially those who have never worked in a business or corporate environment, will find it useful to consult somebody who can help them along their path. No matter how far you think you've got in life, or in business, you will always need feedback, so that you can learn how to do things better. I remind people that even Michael Jackson had a dance coach: somebody whose knowledge he respected, to advise him. If Michael Jackson could be humble enough to seek expert advice, the rest of us mortals need to wise up to the fact that we can benefit from others' experience, too. You will always need somebody around you who knows much more than you do. It's how we learn and grow. For me, Peter Jones is that mentor. But there are others on my team, too, who will share their insights in the chapters that follow.

FIND YOURSELF A BUSINESS MENTOR

Getting somebody on board who knows and understands your business territory will make all the difference to your progress. Mentoring is a wide field. I was lucky to find somebody who excelled in marketing brands as my first mentor. Nadia was also an enthusiastic 'foodie' – so she knew exactly in which direction to point me. Sources for finding a mentor are included on page 278.

My first business mentor: Nadia Jones

Finding Nadia Jones of GLE oneLondon was a stroke of luck for me because I wouldn't usually have had the patience to go searching for funding (see Chapter 2). I thought that there would be too many forms to fill in, too many procedures. My route had been to try the banks first. I prepared endless business plans for them, to try to get the funds via the conventional route because that is what is usually done. After months of trying, the banks had shown no interest in me at all. I had a business plan burning a hole in my pocket, and nowhere else to go with it. I had noticed the adverts for GLE, and I was inspired to go along and make enquiries. What did I have to lose?

Nadia was allocated to me as a business advisor. She saw my passion for my product, she saw that my business plan was strong, and she recognized that it was innovative of me to be saying that I was merging music and food. She also saw the value in the weird product name Reggae Reggae Sauce. Of course, it helped that when she tried it she found that the product tasted good as well. Nadia's advice helped me to raise my game and take my idea to its next level. She showed real commitment and enthusiasm in helping me to work up my idea, even though there was nothing in it for her. That door was open all the time but it could so easily have stayed closed to me had I not woken up to that inspirational feeling and sought advice.

One of the other important lessons in business is that there is always more than one path to follow to get to your destination. There are many routes to achieving your ends. As already mentioned, it is important to learn to step out of your comfort zone and explore doing things differently. Just because you have always done something in a certain way doesn't mean that you have to keep following that same line. Sometimes we need to wake up – or to have someone else wake us up – and say, "This isn't working. Try it another way. Do something else."

By changing my own process and choosing to go down a path that I thought was not for me, I met a talented business person who could help me with my business plan and who started to advise me on where I should go and what I should do next. Nadia's advice to start-ups appears on page 69.

> **You will need a mentor who understands your area of business and can guide you in what to do and who to speak to. See page 275 for further advice on where to find a mentor**

There are Nadias in every field of endeavour, willing to help those who have the passion to make their business happen. But to find such a mentor, you need to be prepared. Make sure that you have already created a business plan, even if it needs further work. Take time to focus on your market and decide on your USP. There is so much information available for free that with some research and a little self-education, a lot of the basics can be prepared in advance. That will leave you mentally prepared to get the deep, specialist advice from your mentor: the nuggets that only those in your industry really know.

Nadia was the first to recognize that the future of business was going to be more about me making my mark with Reggae Reggae Sauce, rather than the sauce itself selling the business. Then, as now, the man is the sauce and the sauce is the business – and the brand.

Even after your business is up and running, you still need to keep on taking good advice. In one sense you never feel as if you have got anywhere in business because there's always more business to do and new things to know.

Few mentors will have anything to gain materially from working with you. There are those, such as Peter Jones, who are both investors and mentors, but usually a mentor is someone who has a desire to help others and wants to give something back. If you do find a good mentor in business, they will most likely be a busy person, and they will have to make the time to work with you. Why would anyone do that? Well, maybe they will see something in you that shows your hunger and your potential; maybe they will have an insight into you as a person and think that you have something and they want to be involved; maybe they will be impressed by your idea and your business plan, and just want to help you make it happen. Whatever their reason, their motivation will be personal, and they will want you to be as committed as they are. The mentor may be motivated by wanting to help, but the mentee will need to feel that there is also a sense of trust.

MONEY, MONEY, MONEY

When I was offered my deal on *Dragons' Den* I felt I had won the lottery. I had spent so many years pitching to banks and looking for the big surplus of cash that would make things easy – and, finally, here it was. But I soon learned that £50,000 was just a drop in the ocean compared with the investment that was needed to get the business off the ground.

Many people believe that "Money is a short cut to success – it means less sweat." Is it, heck! Hard work is what makes the cash. The investment simply opens the first important door.

The start-up phase is very much about planning the long-term view and seeing the bigger financial picture. I had always thought that getting the start-up money for my Reggae Reggae Sauce business was the most important thing I had to do. But it wasn't. What I needed to do was to learn how to *handle* the cash, should I be so lucky as to get my hands on it. I had to learn that money flows fast in business – not *into* your hands, but through and then out of your very clenched fist. Before you know it, your investment is gone and you are left wondering what you have done with it. And what's more, your investors are expecting their slice of the juicy investment cake.

Investment finance is a working commodity: it keeps business on the move and makes things happen. It has a value beyond its monetary worth. But investors invest only if they are likely to see a return on that investment.

Peter Jones has shown me that there are other ways of making your money work for you than by spending it. It is not always necessary to do everything yourself. In the case of Roots Reggae Reggae Sauce Ltd, we chose not to buy a factory, but instead to come to an arrangement with a food manufacturer who already had the necessary facilities. The arrangement works for both companies on a commercial basis, and allows everyone involved to play to their strengths.

The art of money management is a true skill. Chapter 8 tells you more about the nitty-gritty of how to achieve this on a daily and weekly basis. It is one area where you cannot afford to do without advice from a qualified expert. A mentor should be able to help you in this area of money management. Once learned, the method of preserving and budgeting finance and cash flow need never be lost, though you do have to be self-disciplined. First, though, you need to get someone to part with their valuable cash to help you to fulfil your dream.

WHERE WILL THE MONEY COME FROM?

Money can from banks, private investors, friends, family, money lenders – or your own pocket, if you have something you can sell or a house you can remortgage. Some may be tempted to borrow from credit cards and loan sharks – but these are a dangerously expensive route to follow because the interest charged will be extremely high and can wipe out your chances of making a profit before you have even started. The money is not the only important element. Just as important are the terms of the loan and any extra value (such as advice or contacts) that your investor can bring to the table.

In the early days of my business, borrowing from my family was my best option and I will always be grateful to my mother for her early belief in my venture. Borrowing from family won't be an option for everyone, of course, and many people prefer to keep business investment and family separate. But whatever route you choose, the most important thing is to watch the terms and the rate of interest. The cheapest overdraft is the one you don't use.

Remember that people will always want something more from you than you ideally want to give. No one is going to give away anything for free – not even if they are related to you. If you are realistic about that, you won't be surprised or disappointed later.

> At the end of the day, the money is not the most important thing. It's the quality of the business advice and educating yourself on how actually to use the money that is the most important.

KNOW WHEN TO ASK FOR ADVICE

If, like me, you break out in a cold sweat at the very thought of figures, ounces, pounds, and kilos, then this is the point where you need to turn to your advisors. The time for this is *right now*. Find the right advisor to help you to build your business, and the impact on your results will be huge. The improvement in the speed of results will also be enormous. The impact of good advice is the difference between running a business that has you grafting really hard for ten years with little growth to show for all that effort, or developing a business that shows clear growth, year on year. For many people, an excellent ally and starting point may be the bank manager.

Learn to love your bank manager

My early experiences of going to see the bank manager weren't always very positive. Like many would-be entrepreneurs, I tried every bank I could think of with my Reggae Reggae Sauce plan – and I got knocked back every time.

The conversation would go something like this:

"Hello, Mr Bank Manager, Sir, I want to talk to you about getting a loan. I am setting up business for my fabulocious Reggae Reggae Sauce, and I would like some money to fund its development, please."

"Well, Mr Roots… 'Reggie Reggie Sauce': who is Reggie? Is that your name?"

"No, Mr Bank Manager, Sir, it's Reg-gae, Reg-gae Sauce…"

"I'm sorry, Mr Roots, but we don't have the funds available for a venture of that sort. May I wish you a good day."

I couldn't understand it. I was polite, smart, and trying to conform to what I thought was needed. But I fell into the trap that many fall into. I was asking for the loan before I had fully developed my business plan. Most people who are new to business think about borrowing money and getting premises first – which is the wrong way around. It means that they are starting to spend money before they even know whether they are likely to make any. If you talk loan before you talk profit, you will be seen as a high-risk venture.

Your bank manager needs to be involved in your business from day one. He also needs to be able to see that you have done your sales projections, that you have a marketing plan, and that you have budgeted for every stage of the production and delivery process. Your bank manager is all five Dragons in one suit. He or she will want to know that the costings work and that you will stay in close communication with the bank to let them know what is going on.

Luckily, I found success before I found funds – in the form of two business mentors. What Nadia showed me and what I have learned from Peter at a corporate level is that, before anyone will give you any money to spend, you must show that you know how to manage money. Investors need to know that their funds are safe and that you have done your market research. They want to know that you are thinking strategically and aren't just following the crowd. In some ways it is easier to borrow a lot of money than it is to borrow small amounts of money – if the figures add up and the market is there.

In those early days, all I wanted was to get my hands on a loan and get out of there. These days my bank manager is as much a part of the business as my accountant and me.

PAY YOUR DEBTS

It is important to evaluate your living costs before you go into business. Two of the biggest risks to a business are underestimating how much you need for subsistence and borrowing to pay off debt instead of investing money in the business. So pay off your debts *before* you launch your business or it will feel as if you are sinking before you have even started to swim.

It's common sense. Repayment of any business loans – including the interest – must be included in your business plan.

There is another kind of debt to be borne in mind, too. Always remember those who helped you to be successful in the first place. Make sure that you acknowledge them if you pass them on the way up to being a success – because if you do slip, it will be those same hands who will try to help push you back up again. Business fortunes can (and do) go down as well as up – but no one said that it was going to be a smooth ride.

HERE BE DRAGONS

Peter Jones may be in the public eye now, but he hasn't always been. He made his millions long before BBC TV came along and made him a household name. Your business idea may not appear on *Dragons' Den,* but there are Peter Jones–style investors everywhere – in your area, in the whole country, and around the world. You just need to make sure that your figures are prepared and ready, so that you make a good impression on your own personal Dragon when you make your business pitch.

Apparently the early explorers used to write "Here be dragons" on maps to mark unknown territory where they didn't know what to expect. Well, having Dragons on your business plan can be a very good thing. If you have the ambition to plan for outside investment, your business explorations can lead you to exciting new territories where there may be treasure to be found and shared. Here are some tips on how to find and tame your own Dragon, and there is more information on this in Further Resources, page 275.

HOW TO FIND AND TAME AN INVESTMENT DRAGON

Dragons come in all shapes and sizes, but they have two things in common: before they agree to lend you money, they want to know how much profit they are likely to get back (and how quickly) and they want to be sure that their money is in a safe pair of hands. To assess this, they will want to see all of your figures and your sales projections – and to hear your business pitch. All Dragons will want to have some financial input so it is back to the business plan to make sure that it is watertight and up to date. Money can come from several different sources:

Debt finance

A loan or overdraft is called 'debt finance'. It means you start off with a negative before you have even started in business. The advantage of an overdraft over a loan is that you can vary the payments and the amount borrowed yourself and you pay interest only on the amount borrowed.

Watch out for the terms and conditions of any kind of loan agreement. The rate of interest and the timing of the payments can be the sting in the scorpion's tail. A bank may even want you to put up your home as security, which could leave your family very vulnerable.

If you own a house or have some cash saved up, you may be able to use your own capital for the business. But don't forget to leave some for a rainy day – you will lose your flexibility if all your cash is tied up in your business.

You might be lucky enough to get a loan from friends or family. They might not be business-savvy, they might not know anything at all about your area of expertise, but they might believe in you – and so the money may follow. It is an obvious thing to say, but never take undue risks with other people's money, especially if they haven't got much spare to play with. Even family arrangements can go awry, as my brother and I once discovered (see page 175), so it is wise to draw up a formal agreement to avoid any kind of future misunderstanding.

Equity finance

Enter the Dragons; equity finance is their territory. However – as in every fairy story – there is often a twist in the tail. As many have discovered, the television Dragons are really angels in disguise: 'business angels'.

- 'Business angels' are investors who like to invest in fast-growing businesses that are usually SMEs (small- and medium-sized enterprises). They usually invest relatively small sums of money at a time: from £10,000 upwards, but probably not more than £750,000. They will want a share of your company (known as 'equity') and may want to receive financial dividends as income from time to time.
- Venture capitalists are Dragons with big teeth. They have large amounts to invest, often as much as several million pounds at a time. They invest in companies with a proven

track record, so start-up companies will find it harder to be taken seriously. Some of the business Dragons are venture capitalists, too – but that is their day job.

Equity investors will want to know about your 'exit strategy' (your long-term plans for the business) because they will want their money back, together with a good profit (possibly by selling their shares), one day. This may happen quite early on, as in my case when I bought back shares from Richard Farleigh (see page 180).

It may feel strange to be thinking about selling your company before you have even started, but you can't afford to become too emotionally attached. At the end of the day, it is about commercial realities and making a profit.

I always wanted to create a family business and to have a legacy for my children, and that is still my plan. But I have learned that it is not always possible to do that alone. If you want success on a large scale, other people need to be involved as well. Business is all about growth. It is not about standing still.

Grants

A more tempting route for some people may be to apply for a government-funded business grant. This is usually a smaller amount of money (perhaps £1,000). Competition for these types of grants is very fierce, and there are strict terms and conditions to fulfil. Nadia Jones helped me to apply for a grant in the early days, which got me some valuable help with the costs of bottles and labelling. It is a common route for sole traders and smaller start-ups.

But you need to be just as prepared when asking for small sums of money as for large ones, and there is a lot of paperwork to fill in. People will check up on you to make sure that you have stuck to the terms and conditions of the agreement. If you haven't, they will come knocking at your door to get that cash back for someone else.

CHOOSE YOUR INVESTORS WISELY

Not every investor will understand your business – but they may still be willing to invest in you. Peter didn't know anything about Caribbean food, but he could see the potential in the brand, and he knew the people in the business. His first phone call, to Justin King, CEO of Sainsbury's supermarket chain, was the perfect introduction. If you have a sauce to sell, what more do you want than a direct line to the one guy who controls the second-biggest store in the country? It was definitely worth me giving up 20 per cent of the company, just for that phone call!

Of course, not everyone needs a long-term investment Dragon. You may be applying for a grant or have your own equity to get your business off the ground. But whatever your financial arrangements, always choose your business partners wisely. Be careful who you borrow money from, because some of the more ruthless ones could come and bite you in the wallet.

Always have a formal agreement and make sure that you understand the rates of interest and when the money is repayable. Sometimes people are so desperate to get their good idea off the ground that they will borrow from anywhere and anyone to get started – and that could be their downfall in the long run.

> Be very careful who you borrow from – because they could come back and bite you in the wallet.

THE POWER OF A PHONE CALL

Three men were instrumental in getting my sauce on the road. The first two were the original investors: Richard and Peter. But it was Peter's insight to invest, and it was his call to Justin King that really got the Levi Roots Reggae Reggae Foods show on the road. Peter knew Justin of old. He called him up to give him the first opportunity – to say, "Something fantastic is going to happen. Do you want to be a part of it?" As luck would have it, Justin King's son had seen the programme and had already said to him, "Dad, you've got to see this Levi Roots. Get him into Sainsbury's." Before you knew it, as a result of that one phone call, I was meeting Justin and Peter. They were talking about thousands and thousands of bottles of sauce.

At home, my children and I used to make 64 bottles every time we made Reggae Reggae Sauce. That's how many we could get from the metal pot we used for cooking it up. And now, with one phone call, that was about to be increased to *hundreds of thousands* of bottles per batch. Later that first year we sold our first million bottles – and the business has continued to grow ever since.

Not every investor or mentor has a direct line to Justin King – but then again, not every business person wants to grow their business quite so fast. The main thing is that mentoring offers you inroads and information from people who have already been there. Someone could make a call for you or arrange an introduction that could be your own door to business success. Once that door is ajar, it becomes up to you to use your passion, your USP, and your business plan to sell yourself and your brand and push it open.

WHAT HAPPENS NEXT?

Once you have your plan finalized and your finance in place, the next step is to implement that plan and start to make things happen. During the first six months following my deal with Peter and Richard, it was a race off the blocks to get my sauce manufactured and onto the supermarket shelves. I had already set up a company called Roots Reggae Reggae Sauce Ltd and ABF (Associated British Foods PLC) became our business partner on the manufacturing side. ABF is one of the world's largest food companies and produces and supplies food in enormous volume to the supermarkets. I work closely with them to build up the brand identity through marketing and PR.

Those early months were a whirlwind of learning and activity for me. I found myself in a whole range of high-level business meetings, trying to absorb new jargon and information about cash flow and finances as quickly as I could, while also being catapulted into the public eye. Not that I was complaining. My dreams were coming alive at last – and I was enjoying every minute.

> Business jargon and corporate language are among the things people find the most intimidating. My advice is to listen hard to the context of what is being said, and don't try to use the terminology until you are sure you know what the words mean.

The first thing that struck me when I entered the world of corporate business was the language that was being used. Business jargon is an incredible language to get used to. You know that you have arrived when you hear it. In the past when I heard the word 'enterprise', I would always think of *Star Trek*. But enterprise means something completely different in business. Unless you come from a corporate background, you are unlikely to have had words thrown at you to do with business, finance and commercial tactics. They will take some getting used to, but you *will* get used to them. They are only business lyrics. Find out what those words and processes really mean, and keep striding forwards.

The business boardroom is not for everyone. Not everyone has it in them to be a chief. That is why it is important to find out where you sit in the business world. The start-up process shows up many things. For example, you may have a fantastic idea but realize that you are not the perfect person to take it forwards. You may need to prepare to ensure you are the right person to go into the boardroom to secure that contract or that loan.

Take a 'big picture' view from above and weigh things up. Be honest with yourself about your skills, because future success comes down to being true to yourself. It will be *your* hours and *your* money that you will spend. It is all right to look down from above and say, "This is not going to work for me," or to be honest and say, "I've got a fantastic idea but I don't think I am the right person to take it through." Looking from above is a great leveller. If you are honest with yourself, you will make the right decisions about what your strengths are, where you need others to act for you, and who you need to team up with to make things happen.

> Be honest with yourself about your skills, because future success comes down to being true to yourself. It will be your hours and your money that you will spend.

MAKING YOUR BUSINESS OFFICIAL

You have your plan. You have done your market research.
You are raring to go. But there is one more thing you need to
do before you get started – because this is the point when
your business starts to become official. You need to tell
HMRC (Her Majesty's Revenue & Customs) and possibly
Companies House that you are setting up a business, so
that you exist officially and so that you benefit from the
concessions that are available for companies during the
start-up phase.

So here is the nitty-gritty of what it's all about. This is
just basic information. Many of the Further Resources (see
page 275) will give you more detail, and, of course, your
accountant will help you, too. You will be fined if you do
not tell HMRC about your business within a certain number
of days, so don't be tempted to put off this stage.

A business can trade in one of three ways:
• As a sole trader
• As a limited company
• As a business partnership

Any type of business turning over more than £70,000 a year
will have to register for VAT (unless your business is exempt).
And any business can employ people, but will have to take
out employers' liability insurance and run a payroll system for
PAYE and national insurance (or get an accountant to do it).

Sole traders

If you set up business on your own you will be a sole trader. This is the simplest business structure and could be the right choice if you want to keep start-up costs low.

You will need to register as self-employed with HMRC and keep accounts so that you can file a self-assessment tax return each year. You will have to pay personal income tax on your profits.

The main disadvantage of being sold trader is that if things go wrong you will be personally liable for all the debts of the business.

Partnership

If two or more people go into business together (without setting up a company) they will be entering into a partnership. This is like being a sole trader, except that there are two or more people carrying on the business.

Each person must register as self-employed with HMRC and file a self-assessment tax return each year and pay income tax on their individual share of the profits. The partnership also has to file its own tax return, but doesn't pay any tax.

It is important that you agree with your partners at the outset, in a written agreement, all of the commercial arrangements for a partnership.

It is important that you agree with your partners at the outset, in a written agreement, all of the commercial arrangements for the partnership such as:

• What business you are going to carry on
• How much money are each of you going to invest into the business
• How you will share the profits or losses
• How much time each of you must give to the business
• What happens if one of you wants to leave

And like a sole trader, if things go wrong each of the partners will be personally liable for all of the debts of the business.

A limited company

A limited company is incorporated by registering it at Companies House (or you could buy an 'off the shelf' company that has already been registered from a company formation agent).

Legally a registered company is regarded as a separate 'person' from its shareholders and directors. This means that it can have bank accounts, own property, enter into contracts in its own name, and can live forever. A company has to register with HMRC and prepare annual tax returns, and keep accounts and file them each year at Companies House.

A company pays corporation tax on its profits, and can pay its after-tax profits to shareholders as dividends. Shareholders (except basic rate taxpayers) then pay income tax on those dividends as part of their own income.

If you are running a company it is very important to keep the company's finances total separate from your own.

A main advantage of a company is that the shareholders liability is limited to the amount they invested for their shares, even if the business fails. Investors are more willing to invest in a company than to enter into a partnership where their personal liability is unlimited.

If you bring in outside investors you will need a shareholders' agreement, setting out the arrangements for their investments and their rights in the company.

A company is run by its directors (in a small company these will usually be the same people as the shareholders). The directors have heavy legal responsibilities to make sure that the company is run properly. They can be made personally liable for the company's debts if they breach those obligations and if the company goes into liquidation.

In all instances it is wise to ask for legal and financial advice when setting up in business with someone else. See Teja Picton Howell's advice on pages 183–197.

> A main advantage of a company is that the shareholders liability is limited to the amount they invested for their shares, even if the business fails.

A LITTLE WORD ABOUT VAT

Value Added Tax is charged on most goods and services that you buy. If you are a trader registered for VAT you charge VAT on the goods or services you supply (unless those goods or services are 'zero rated' - ie the VAT rate is 0%). Every three months you will have to fill in and file a VAT return and declare all the VAT you have charged (your VAT 'outputs') and all the VAT you have paid (your VAT 'inputs'). If you have charged more VAT than you have paid you have to pay the difference to HMRC. But if you have paid more VAT than you have charged, you can claim a refund for the difference. If your turnover is more than £70,000 per year you will have to register for VAT (unless your business is 'VAT exempt'). There can be advantages in registering for VAT voluntarily if your turnover is less than £70,000, because if you are paying more VAT then you're charging you may be able to claim back the difference. VAT returns and any payments due have to be made within the month after the end of each VAT period.

CHOOSING AND REGISTERING A COMPANY NAME OR TRADEMARK

Choosing a company name is one of the most fun and important things you will do when starting up your business. As a general rule, make sure that the name is memorable and instantly recognizable by the customer and tells them what they need to know. It is probably as well to avoid unusual spellings that could be hard to remember or search online.

There are a number of rules and guidelines that govern the choice of company names. For example, there are certain 'sensitive' words that may not be used without permission from the Registrar of Companies, or other authority, such as 'royal'; words that must be used with care, which imply a service or a certain status, such as 'association' or 'national'; or words that imply a function, such as 'charity'. A limited company must always include 'Limited' or the letters 'Ltd' at the end of its name. These kinds of details can be checked on the Companies House website (see Further Resources, page 275).

When choosing a name for your company, be careful not to choose a name that has already been registered as a trademark, or as a company at Companies House, or which might be confusing with the name of an existing business. It's easy to do your research now on the Companies House and Intellectual Property Office websites, and by carrying out Google searches.

> As a general rule, make sure that your company name is memorable and instantly recognizable by the customer and tells them what they need to know.

If you want to sell overseas, you will need to check in all the territories you are planning to trade in. As already mentioned, if you are a limited company you will need to register the name with Companies House. A name should also be checked via the Trade Marks Register. The easiest way to do this is to search the online index of company names at the Intellectual Property Office.

Tips for choosing a company name:

- Choose something that is simple and memorable.
- Register the name with all relevant bodies.
- Register the name and logo of your company as a trademark.
- Remember that every registered company must display their company name in a prominent position.
- Sole traders must not imply that they have limited or partnership status.
- Company names must not be offensive.
- Check out the general rules and guidelines online at Companies House.

KEEP THINGS SIMPLE

The secret of growing your business is to keep things simple, and to begin by thinking local. Many people who find it hard to get their business off the ground are trying to fly before they can walk or are making things too complicated. The big picture is important, but if you make that picture *too* big, you won't be able to see your feet to take your first steps.

Trying to do too much too soon or creating a business plan that is over-complicated often stops people from moving forward at all. For example, planning to expand overseas before you have established your business locally will overstretch you and cause you to make expensive mistakes, instead of allowing time to learn from the smaller, localized ones. Sourcing goods from developing markets, looking at overseas distribution, talking about expansion plans, and so on are good to have in the plan for the long term. But at the start-up stage it is more important to be dealing with suppliers you can visit and talk to, who can offer you flexibility on terms if needs be, and who will deliver fast if necessary. Unless you are ordering or selling on such a large scale that sourcing overseas will make a difference to your costs, it is better to keep your focus local, so you are in control of the supply chain and can keep things smooth and easy.

> Have the confidence to know that there are lots of other businesses that have done something similar to what you have in mind. You just need the drive and ambition to stick at it and stay focused.

Running a business is not rocket science. Hundreds of millions of people of every age are running businesses around the world every minute of every day. You are not reinventing the wheel: there is so much information already out there that you can learn from. The internet is full of information, there are books and videos about other people's experiences, and there is more help for enterprise and start-ups than ever before. Have the confidence to know that there are lots of other businesses out there that have done something similar to what you have in mind. You just need the drive and ambition to stick at it and stay focused. The most important thing is to do what you have planned to do, and what you know you can do, and to do it very well.

You have to start by testing your market, and it makes sense to start with those you know, who will give you honest feedback and be a bit more forgiving if a few mistakes are made along the way.

DON'T LET ANYBODY STOP YOU

If you feel that other people are holding you back, the truth is that *you* are most likely the main problem. Avoid complacency. Keep your foot on the accelerator at all times – especially at the start-up stage when an ability to self-motivate can be a vital asset.

FROM AN INVESTOR'S PERSPECTIVE

Investors want to be won over by the leadership style and the vision of the business owner. There can be nothing more soul-destroying for an entrepreneur than to have their plans scuppered because they fail to give a strong account of themselves or are ill-prepared for the questions asked. Noone is obliged to invest in your business or lend you money. No matter how brilliant you believe your concept to be, you need to be able to sell your idea and to prove that you have done your groundwork. Success depends upon adequate preparation.

Investors will want you to respect their time and will expect your pitch to be well rehearsed. This is all-important. Ask someone you trust to critique your performance honestly in advance so that you are 'pitch perfect' before you go to your meetings. Eat, sleep, and breathe your financial data and your forecasts. If the facts and figures are second nature, you will be free to be yourself, and your presentation will be more natural and more professional.

A BRILLIANT IDEA: An investor needs to feel enthused about the product or service that is being pitched. Make sure you can summarize your business benefits in a sentence.

A SNAPSHOT OF THE BUSINESS: Offer a short statement about your vision and values – and your USP.

WHAT'S THE STORY? Tell the investor what has brought you to this point. Have you had to sell your house? Have you run a business in the past? What have you had to give up, to get this far? Your story displays your values and your tenacity. Investors like people who have the inner toughness to keep going through challenging times.

YOUR TRACK RECORD: Investors are impressed by entrepreneurs who have a track record of success, who have shown they are capable of selling and marketing their idea or product, who get repeat business, and who can make sound commercial decisions.

HOW MUCH? Explain how much you want to borrow, what you will be spending it on, and why. Be honest. Your argument will seem flawed if you cannot answer questions consistently.

MARKET ANALYSIS: No investor will part with their capital for an idea that has not been thoroughly researched. Talk about the size and potential of the chosen marketplace, including accurate facts and figures about demographics, competitor analysis, forward trends, and so on.

RETURN ON INVESTMENT (ROI): An investor needs to know that their resources are in safe hands and that there is a strategy in place to ensure there is likely to be a profit. Your plan should clearly show projected ROI and this needs to be supported by evidence, such as the research data, the potential risks, the market knowledge, and the size of the market. A business will flourish or die according to the rigour of the business plan and the accuracy of the sales and cash flow forecasting.

COMMUNICATION SKILLS: Your presentation needs to be polished, engaging, and well prepared. Keep it clear, concise, compelling, and coherent. Successful investors will see through unnecessary filler. Anchor your pitch with essential facts but don't overuse PowerPoint or you will lose people's attention. Make sure that you look and sound the part, too. Courtesy, body language, and being smartly dressed are equally important forms of communication.

PERSONAL FIRE AND CHARISMA: Show your personality. Successful businesses are run by those who can lead, inspire, and influence others. People are investing in you as much as in the business.

It's not about liking or disliking, it's about recognizing business acumen.

MOTIVATION AND COMMITMENT: It is not enough to want to make money in business, there needs to be another motive, too. My true motivation was to build a good life for my children. Personal motivation drives the level of commitment you feel for the business.

BEING A TEAM PLAYER: Tucking yourself away in an office for 10 hours a day and trying to be completely self-reliant will not take you very far in business. To make things happen, you need to work with others who have the knowledge and experience you lack.

FINANCIAL RELIABILITY: The investor will always run a series of credit checks and will also go through the figures in some detail before signing a deal.

A MUTUALLY BENEFICIAL ARRANGEMENT: You need to make sure that the arrangement works for you, too. You need to feel that the investor is the 'right' business partner for your future plans and that they are fully engaged and understand what you are aiming to achieve. Keep the lines of communication fully and honestly open.

You owe it to the investor to safeguard their money to the best of your ability – and they may well insist on having some form of equity or influence within your company. Nevertheless, as long as you own the majority share, you should feel free to stay true to your own vision of the future.

Of course, not everything works out quite as planned, and you won't always win straight away the investment you seek. Don't be disheartened if you get turned down a few times.

Assess what may have let you down, ask for feedback, and make adjustments. If you are determined enough and you have a watertight and commercial concept, you will eventually find a backer.

CHAPTER 5

STANDING OUT –
HOW TO MAKE YOUR MARK

Roots of success 5:
Make yourself and your business special

*"It's so nice I had to name it twice.
I called it Reggae Reggae Sauce."*

LEVI ROOTS

Marketing a product or service is all about telling a story and telling it at the right time. This involves getting a message across, engaging with people, and helping them to understand clearly what you are telling them and why. Every time I talk about Reggae Reggae Sauce or any of the other products in my brand range, I link it to my *Dragons' Den* story because many people felt a part of that experience, which makes the brand more personal.

You can do this with your own brand, too. Explain it in a way that will draw other people in and make them understand how it is relevant to them and their lives. Whether you are opening a shop, developing a service, or manufacturing a product, there is always a story and there is always something that will make you stand out and make your business special. Building a brand is about building a lasting relationship with those you do business with (your business partners or customers), as well as your customers or end users. This chapter covers how to build a brand and how to make your pitch, and offers broader guidance on how to use marketing to make yourself and your business special.

BUSINESS IS A TRUE PERFORMANCE

In Jamaica we talk about "fixing up your shop", which means making the best of yourself. No matter how humble your beginnings, there is no excuse for not appearing clean and fresh and smartly turned out. This is especially true for one-man bands and people who are operating on a small scale. All you have to represent your company is yourself and your brand. You have to make that shine.

Every time you go out and represent your company, you must be ready to give your best, even if you're not feeling particularly on form. You have to present at 100 per cent *always* because you're always on show.

You are your brand or products. People invest in people. Whatever you are trying to sell, you have to sell yourself with it. The ways you dress, speak, communicate with other people, and so on, portray a message. Every time you choose what to wear or open your mouth to say something, you are representing your business and your brand. It is important to remember that. Even when you are relaxing, you are still on show. Who knows who you might meet on the train or when you are socializing that could open up a whole new strand of business opportunities? Make sure that whomever you meet will want to be associated with you and what you have to offer. You have to stay true to your best self at all times.

As mentioned earlier, your foot always has to be on the accelerator. There is a bright and positive reason for this. If you're at your best, it means that you will already be prepared and ready for the next opportunity when it presents itself. You won't have to stop to think about it.

> What you wear and what you say represent your business and your brand. Even when you are relaxing, you are still on show. Be your best self, always.

'Lively up yourself'

On *Dragons' Den*, my pal Peter Jones has a pet hate. He gets profoundly irritated by people who come on the show dressed casually or in jeans. He feels so strongly about this that if some guy is not wearing a tie Peter won't invest in a perfectly good business opportunity worth millions of pounds. "Come on!" you might say, "What is that about?" It's about Peter's personal values and his business identity. Because it won't be Peter who has blown the opportunity – it will be the guy who didn't think about what Peter is looking for. Peter Jones wants everyone and everything associated with his brand to be a good representation of his company, and he will look to reinforce that with every investment. His investments have to reflect *him* – and that's why he will invest. He'll want you to be a brand ambassador for his name.

Wherever I go, I represent Peter. I am an extension of him and the group of companies he has worked so hard and for so long to build up. The opposite applies, too: he is doing that for me. When he talks about the Reggae Reggae companies, it has to be in the same way as I would talk about them. The core message about the sunshine flavours of the Caribbean and putting music in your food has to be the same, whether he says it or I do. You have to be consistent. The way you speak and the way you represent the brand are very important.

MAKING YOUR PITCH

That brings me on to making your pitch. The day I met
the Dragons with my guitar and my song, I put on a
performance of a lifetime. Everything I had ever learned
during my musical career came together for me at that
moment. When I walked up those stairs, I wasn't performing
to Peter Jones and his Dragon colleagues – in my mind I
was performing to a packed crowd at Wembley stadium.
I knew that I needed to put on an Oscar-winning
performance to win them over.

No performance before or since has ever been as
nerve-racking – but I know that every performance in a
business meeting is just as important. I treat all business
people with the same amount of respect as I did the
Dragons. I prepare more thoroughly these days as well
because my figures very nearly let me down that day.

Preparation and planning

One of the reasons that so many people fail when they go
on *Dragons' Den* is because they haven't fully prepared.
I didn't really know the format of the show, but believe
me when I say that I thought my pitch had been well
rehearsed. I had written my song at the same time as
my business plan; I had been cooking up a business
in my kitchen long before the day I tried to win over
those hard-nosed business tycoons;and I had pitched
for funding more times than I can remember. But I
nearly blew it – because I hadn't learned my numbers
off by heart.

When I asked for the investment of £50,000 in exchange for 20 per cent of my business, I backed that up by telling them that I had got a very nice order from a meat company in Yorkshire for *2½ million litres* of sauce. I had taken the confirmation letter with me, too, as part of the 'due diligence' process.

Dragon number one, Deborah Meaden, wanted to know about my plans for the investment and whether I had taken advice on how to produce the sauce in the volume I was talking about. I told her that I would rent premises for £25,000 and hire the necessary equipment. She didn't agree with the strategy, and so I knew that she would be out.

Dragon number two, Duncan Bannatyne, hadn't even tried the sauce, so I didn't hold out much hope there.

But Richard Farleigh had been tapping his toes to my song, and as Dragons go, number three looked friendly – though I will never forget the cold feeling around my heart when I heard him say, "There is something I don't understand… You've got an order for 2½ *thousand* kilos of sauce. That is not 2½ *million* litres, that is 2½ *thousand* litres."

I got very confused. "That's 250,000 litres isn't it?" But it wasn't. It was 2,500 litres. 1 kilo = 1 litre. Oh dear.

Then they said, "You're getting £6.50 per litre?" I confirmed that I was. That was about £130,000 per year. A big difference from what I had suggested. Deborah and Duncan were out.

Theo Paphitis's next words cut through me like a knife: "That letter *is not an order* – and it is a hugely difficult and complicated business to get into major supermarkets… *you've got very little hope.*" Dragon number four went fast.

At that moment I thought it was all over. I could see my spirit hovering above my body, slain by Dragons and lying on the floor of the television studio.

But Peter had reread the letter and noticed that 2,500 litres was the initial requirement. Thereafter there was a potential order for 500 kilos per week. The dawn was breaking. Richard noted that was a potential 25,000 kilos a year – which was a turnover of more than £160,000.

"You would probably admit that your business skills need a little bit of help," said Richard. Well, that was certainly true. Fortunately for me, he was starting to see a spark of potential.

Then Peter spoke up. "To try and range one product is nearly impossible," he said, pausing dramatically. "But I like impossible challenges! I don't know whether it's the sauce that I have just taken, or what I am about to say…" What *was* he about to say?

"I will offer you half the money – for 20 per cent."

Peter's promise to call the CEO of Sainsbury's, clinched the deal and made up Richard's mind. Richard put up the rest of the money for another 20 per cent.

I took a little moment at the back of the hall to consider my options. I had come into the Den to bargain with 20 per cent of my business for £50,000. They wanted to give me the money – but they wanted 40 per cent of the business, which was more than I wanted to give away. Always be careful when you negotiate terms – because the other person will always want more than you are willing to give. Know what your high and low points are – before you begin to bargain.

While I stood there, weighing up my options, something that my mother had said to me came back to me: "It's better to have less of a business that is going somewhere fast than to have 100 per cent of something that is going nowhere." Sixty per cent of something backed by two millionaire investors could turn into quite a lot. It became an easy decision to make.

Money could not buy the worth of the expertise that Peter has given to the business since then. Money couldn't have paid for the value of Richard saying, "Yes, I am going to invest" on national TV. The extra 20 per cent that I had to give away bought me an extra Dragon – and overnight recognition for my brand.

In spite of all that, when I watched the episode back at home with my family the next day, we were still not sure whether I would win the deal!

Peter Jones said something else to me that day: "I like you, Levi, and I think that your sauce is great, too. I wouldn't buy (it) if it wasn't you selling it to me." That was quite something to hear because it was a reminder that people (even Dragons) always buy from people. So brush off your charisma and polish up your likeability factor. Remember that you are your brand – and anything is possible.

> People buy from people. Remember that you are your brand – and anything is possible.

LEVI'S TOP TIPS FOR MAKING A WINNING PITCH

- Know your USP.
- Practise getting your core message across clearly in less than one minute.
- Know your numbers and learn the lingo. If you are asked questions, you need to be able to answer them knowledgeably.
- Think about what you may be asked, and be prepared.
- Look smart.
- Breathe and relax.
- Speak slowly – and pause between points – to give people time to absorb what you are saying.
- If you lose your way, stop and ask a question to give yourself thinking time.
- Invite questions and listen carefully to what people have to say.
- Give yourself time to think before you answer.
- Stay calm and polite at all times. Avoid becoming challenging or defensive.
- Know what deal you will agree to before the negotiation begins.
- Be honest.
- Be true to yourself.

Check details ahead of time

These days, my team and I will go over every detail before we pitch to a customer, and we send the paperwork in advance, so that if there are any queries they can be raised ahead of the main meeting. You can be sure that I make sure I know the figures – and I will take someone with me who is better versed in maths than I will ever be.

Get everything together in advance. This is a day for paying attention to the details and being prepared. Don't leave *anything* to chance.

• Be sharp-suited with polished shoes. You don't need to be wearing designer labels to make a good impression, but you need to make sure there is not a crease out of place.

• Get your hair trimmed if you need to. Now is not the time for the holiday look.

• If you are travelling any distance, book your travel tickets or taxi in advance, or plan your driving route.

• Take the name, address, contact number, and a map with you. You don't want to risk being late because you headed the wrong way down the road.

• Give yourself plenty of time. If you know that you leave things to the last minute or that you are always rushing, add an hour to your journey time. And leave on time.

• Get everything ready the night before. Have your presentation materials ready and in a folder, make sure your clothes are sharp, and put everything from your keys to your mobile phone together so that you don't forget anything.

• Make sure you know your figures inside out – you will need to be able to answer questions quickly and without rustling lots of papers.

PERFECTING THE IMAGE

Your brand is represented not only by the way you dress and speak – the message also needs to be consistent every time you write an email, make a phone call, or give someone a business card, and every time a customer clicks onto your website. Your website, your business cards, and your social media pages (such as Facebook, LinkedIn, or Twitter) should all present you so that, every time anyone reads about you or sees something to do with your company, they reinforce the message and that person understands, at a deep level, what you stand for and what you will deliver.

Protect your brand identity

One of the most important roles of my legal advisor is to make sure that our business partners understand how to use the Levi Roots brand and the logo. Every detail is included in the licensing agreement, including the Pantone colours of the logo, the style and size of the font, and where they should go on the packaging.

The Levi Roots logo is about representing me and my music. I wanted my guitar to feature on everything we produced. The team at Sainsbury's wanted my face on there, too. The sunshine colours reflect the feel-good nature of the brand and all that it stands for.

If design is not your thing, it will be a new skill to learn. Think of any brand you use or respect, then look at its website, packaging, stationery, or the way it signs off its emails. Everything will be standardized; everything will reinforce the message.

Your business card says a lot about you

When people come up to me to talk about their business, the first thing I will ask for is a business card. If they don't have one, I say, "Come back to me when you have one. Until then you are wasting my time because you are not taking yourself, or me, seriously." You must have a business card – and the look of your card is important.

In Japan the business card is considered to represent the person at all times and is treated with great respect. It is received with two hands and always remains on the table throughout the meeting. (This is a good idea. It means you can have a sneaky look at it while you are talking, to remind you of the name of the person and the company!)

People keep business cards. They are an easy route to future business. But remember that, when people look at your business card, they will notice if it is badly designed or has been run off cheaply. If your budget is small and your only route is to use a ready-made template, keep your design simple and distinctive. Include on the card the following information:

• Your contact information: name, address, phone number, and email.

- Your web address (if you have one).
- Your USP. People collect hundreds of business cards. Your USP will remind them of who you are, and it will reinforce the memory of your brand in their mind.

The wonder of the web

The internet is a wonderful tool for getting your message out to the world in less time than it takes to say, "Reggae Reggae Sauce". But it is a world that is becoming increasingly sophisticated.

If I am about to do business with someone, you can be sure that I will go online and check them out. If I look at their website and it's not up to much, I'm going to doubt their business acumen. A notice reading "Website under construction" or a bad website is often worse than having none at all.

If you are setting up meetings or are meeting with prospective customers, they will probably do some research on you via the Web, too: looking not just at your website, but also at news pages and other sources. It's the first point of call. Google yourself and see what you can find. The Web has a long memory. Is there anything there? Is it all positive? If not, how can you change that?

Blogs and the like are potentially great for your PR. But make sure that you are always being yourself and coming across positively and with a consistent message.

Standing out and being noticed isn't just about getting attention – it is about communicating, too, with people of different age groups and backgrounds. Think outside the box in everything you do, and consider how you can use every opportunity to build a good news story about your business.

Making the most of PR

The instant that I walked up the stairs into *Dragons' Den* I appeared in nearly five million sitting rooms across the country. That made it worth all the anxiety of the day. You cannot have better PR than television. Having that level of publicity has an associated value for other companies, so, not surprisingly, since that time I have been approached by several major businesses interested in using the Levi Roots brand.

Unexpected opportunities will show the true value of having a plan. As a snapshot reminder of what you are about, it prevents you from being sidetracked on a path that has the potential to distract from the main market and the core plan.

My personal philosophy is: "Put some music in your food." It represents everything that I am: a fusion of my culture, my influences, and my passions. The companies' USP is built on this. The Reggae Reggae Group is concerned with raising the profile of Caribbean food and culture. If Levi Roots wouldn't cook it, eat it, or wear it, then it is not right for the company. The objective is to keep people's focus on all things Caribbean, so that those who are new to it will understand what we are about, and those from the Caribbean community can keep the vibe.

This means that foods such as baked beans, noodles or chips are out in the short term – even though they would sell and we would make money from them. At the moment, that is not our objective. In the long term, who knows? A plan is a guideline, not a straitjacket. We have lots of other ideas for the future.

> When anyone looks at a Levi Roots product or any of our marketing material, they will see the sunshine colours, they will see our branding and our typography, and they will see my USP because every box reads: "Put some music in your food." They will also notice that everything is delivered with "OneLove" from Levi Roots.

BUILDING A RELATIONSHIP WITH YOUR CUSTOMERS

As a start-up entrepreneur, you need to understand who your customers are and what they want. If you are pitching to a retailer or a supermarket, do your research in advance so that you understand how they categorize their products. Try to get some consumer data on what the highest turnover items are. You can get this information from company websites, a business library, the company's annual report – or just by asking nicely!

> It's a cliché, but it is true: your customers are your business.

I am still very much involved in the music business, although I don't have as much time for gigs these days. I started off with just a few fans, and over the years I've built that fan base into a much bigger one. These fans have told their friends about my music, so that now I have a steady following of Levi Roots fans, who will always buy whatever music I put out there. Those fans have grown with me. They are loyal to me and my 'brand', and I appreciate them for that.

We have taken a similar approach to growing the Reggae Reggae range. The Caribbean community was there with me from the start, at the Notting Hill Carnival, and they still come back each year. The queues get longer and longer. We have dedicated sauce users, too, who will willingly try our other products. Every section of the market is consciously geared to bringing a new set of customers to the sunshine table.

Timing is everything

Retailers organize their products into different categories. In the case of food, the divisions are condiments (including sauces), frozen foods (including chargrills and burgers), ready meals, fresh foods, seasonal foods, and so on.

If you want to pitch your product to a retail chain in the hope that they will stock it and sell it to their High Street customers, you need to think about which season is likely to be best for marketing and find out about their buying cycle.

For example, in the clothing industry, winter clothes are pitched to the chain stores in the spring and are in the shops while the sun is still shining in late summer – well before you really need them. The designers and manufacturers must make sure that the fashion and lifestyle magazines have what they need for marketing features at least two months ahead of the publication date.

The food business is similar. Levi Roots Reggae Reggae Food products are associated with the barbecue season, so if we aren't geared up to pitch the new range at the beginning of the buying cycle, we will have missed our 'window of opportunity', and we might as well wait until the following year.

Every industry has its sales cycle and its marketing and PR machine, and it is important to be well organized so that advance information about your product is ready at the right time. That means there needs to be a separate sales sheet for every sauce or range, every ready meal, every frozen meal, and the same goes for other industries such as books, toys, and gardening equipment.

Every product needs a USP

A retailer will want to be able to understand the USP of the product or brand that is being presented within each category, before they will decide to stock it. It needs to be clear to consumers, too, and give both new and existing consumers a reason to pick it up.

Supermarkets, in particular, want to see a brand that truly excites the consumers of that category, persuading them to spend more. The buyers will ask: Why should I list this brand? What does it add to the category? Will it bring new consumers into the category? Will it make current consumers pick up two bottles instead of one? What kind of marketing and PR support are being provided to support our sales efforts?

When you are planning your strategy, aim for maximum market penetration. You have to be strategic about it, so save the 'nice-to-haves' until later. Find that point of difference, and try to add some excitement to the sector you are going into.

In a company like mine, where people and contacts are on more than one site, it is also important to make sure that members of your team keep talking to one another. As the business owner, you will need to make sure that the message you want communicated *outside* the company is kept consistent across every department and across every form of communication *inside* the company, too.

What can you do for free?

A common mistake when you are starting out is to start spending more extravagantly than you need to. There has never been a better time to get marketing for free. Before spending on leaflets, mailshots, etc, think about the customers you are aiming at. Are they a section of the market that will use the internet?

I think sometimes, when people are starting up, they get preoccupied with appearance. You don't necessarily need to start spending out on premises and mailshots. Could you operate from home for a while? Could you do some door-to-door or telephone selling? It's a great way to get to know what your customers really want. I used to walk about selling my sauce from a rucksack on my back. I knew all my customers personally. As far as possible, I still do that today. I will always do a presentation to the sales team of whichever company is selling my products, and I spend a lot of time touring the country cooking up a storm at food fairs and other events.

I am not on a mission just to build my company – as I have said before, I want Caribbean food to become as popular as other cuisines such as Chinese and Indian food. And that takes hard graft.

ADVICE FOR BUSINESSES OWNERS WHO WANT TO GET NOTICED

The following tips are based on marketing manager Shah Khan's strategy for our brand:

Universal positivity: You don't have to be Levi Roots to become a living embodiment of your brand Work closely with everyone who interacts with your brand at every level, to ensure universal positivity and a shared vision. You're not selling just to the end consumer – you're also selling to the retailer's buyers who sell the product and to the people who make the product.

Understand your retailers: Build a fantastic relationship with your retailers, so that you always understand their needs and motivations.

Talk to your consumers: Live and breathe your brand and target consumer. Always know what consumers think about your brand and how it makes them behave. Build a strong, lasting relationship with them.

Always look at the return on any marketing investment: People can get carried away with spending money quite freely. Prioritize, and make sure that any investment has a positive return. If you're spending £1 on marketing, make sure that you make more than £1 in profit. You will need to either be able to increase your margins by putting up your prices or sell a lot more. Look at the bigger value on any return, too: where the sales are coming from, who is buying, when, and why.

Don't lose sight of the finances: The financial return on your marketing investment, and the reach and impact of your PR coverage, are crucial to your success.

Pay attention to the story: You might have done a PR campaign that had fantastic reach and fantastic PR value, but you need to make sure that what people are writing about is all positive, too! A negative story can undermine all your investment and damage the equity of your brand.

Get consumer feedback: When we put together the first Subway sandwich campaign, we wanted to target the 16–30 market, and we also needed to develop something that would bring Reggae Reggae Sauce to the attention of a large number of our target audience. The Reggae Reggae Chicken Sub launch successfully answered both objectives. The aim was to excite consumers with a memorable marketing campaign, something that would give the brand good visibility. The fun nature of the advertising, especially the posters, was fantastic. Subway ran this campaign each summer for two years and ran it for eight weeks through the first summer. If your campaign swallows a large chunk of money, you will want to test any creative idea on your target audience before and after you've run it. They may tell you that they loved the campaign and they can't wait to see it again, though they may have suggestions for what you could do differently. Don't take any negative reactions at surface value. Find out the reasons behind them and address them.

Act swiftly to build momentum, and keep that momentum going: Trailblazers need to move quickly if they are to stay ahead of the pack.

Sell, sell, sell: This is always key. In the first year of launch, you have to really engage everyone you come into contact with and you interact with, at every level. Focus and communicate your USP far and wide. However, if you keep doing the same thing the same way, people will stop noticing it, so it is important to keep a fresh approach.

Market saturation occurs when a product loses its freshness factor and people get a little bored with it. Watch out for the triggers that you need to start doing things a little differently. We aim at different markets with different products; however, when we aim at the youth market, we know we have to be constantly setting the trend, rather than following it.

Be flexible in approach: The 16–30 age group, which is our core audience, is inundated with a lot of brands and a lot of messages. They are very fickle and will switch brands and usage very quickly. Although we always offer a consistent message, we also try to do something that captures their imagination and is quite unconventional. We always aim to do something that is exciting and will make the consumer think slightly differently.

Anticipate new trends: By getting to know your consumers so well and seeing how they behave, it is possible to make reasonable assumptions about what they might like. It's like looking into a crystal ball.

Reframe the past: There are lots of products out there that haven't worked first time around because they were ahead of their time, but it doesn't mean they can't have a new lease of life. Perhaps there is a different way of raising visibility; maybe the target audience was wrong or usage and application needed development.

Build brand ambassadors: One of the reasons that Levi Roots the brand has worked so well is word-of-mouth marketing and recommendation. When this works, it can have far more impact than press or TV advertising. Of the many TV adverts that are shown, you may remember only a handful, whereas with user-generated YouTube videos or Facebook groups you achieve real cut-through by getting genuine consumer interaction. This form of viral marketing is a way of getting your consumers to do your job for you.

A BRAND-NEW DIMENSION

Every brand needs a man like Shah. He is full of great ideas and has the energy and enthusiasm to push things forward as if his life depends on it. He has as much belief in the Levi Roots brand as I do, and we work together closely to come up with new concepts. His responsibility is to push and drive the brand as far as it will go, to come up with new ideas – and to keep being creative.

When you are starting up, you will be your own brand manager. But you will also find allies within the companies you are working with. Make it your business to fire up the people with whom you have business dealings. Share your ideas with them and help them to help you to take your business forward.

Shah Khan, senior brand manager

"As senior brand manager for the Levi Roots brand, I have the exciting job of working with Levi to bring his vision to life. We are on a mission to bring his fun, vibrant Caribbean flavours to the people of the UK – and, in time, the rest of the world. This means having a deep understanding of Levi's aims and core brand values, and focusing on getting his message out to the mass market.

People ask me what makes Reggae Reggae Sauce and the associated products such a success: I tell them it is because of Levi, the man. People can relate to Levi Roots. He lives like everybody else does: he walks the streets, rides on the bus – though maybe not quite as often these days! Levi *is* the brand. People feel that they can reach out to Levi and communicate with him; he is accessible. It is fantastic for me to have a living, breathing brand to work with, but it is great for the consumer, too, because it adds a whole new dimension to what they experience when they taste Levi's food.

People will always remember Levi as 'the Reggae Reggae sauce man with the song'. The association will never go away, and it's not something that we want to go away. People connect with Levi through his success. Without *Dragons' Den* and without Peter Jones, there would be no story. But it is only one chapter of a much longer story: there is a lot more to Levi Roots than a day of Dragon-slaying.

What Levi did with his sauce and his original marketing pitch was a work of pure genius. His sauce was already unique, but using the song and his music to bridge the culture gap – and deliver a clear marketing message – was just brilliant.

'Put some music in your food…' That song tells you about Levi, it tells you what is in the sauce, what it's called, how it tastes, and what to do with it – and the lyrics stay in your mind for days, even weeks. It is genius!"

> ❛ What Levi did with his sauce and his original marketing pitch was a work of genius. It was a strategy that could not have been devised by anyone else. ❜

Put some music in my food for me
Reminds people of the USP
Gimme some reggae reggae sauce
Tells you Levi likes it
Hot reggae reggae sauce
Tells people what it is
It's so nice I had to name it twice
Explains the name
I called it reggae reggae sauce
Repeats it so people get the message
Hot reggae reggae sauce
Now people really get it!
Just like my baby it's the perfect delight
Makes it sound irresistible
It's got some peppers and some herbs and spice
Explains the ingredients
We want some reggae reggae sauce
Hints at the demand
Hot reggae reggae sauce
Reinforces
So nice with your fried chicken Makes burgers finger-licking
On rice and peas and fish
Tells you what to do with it
Put some reggae reggae sauce on your lips
Reinforces the whole message

HOW TO BUILD A LIVE BRAND

"At the time of the launch of Reggae Reggae Sauce, the PR coverage about 'Levi the Dragon-slayer' was far and wide, so in the first year we launched a three-pronged approach to building the equity of the brand, which Levi endorsed whole-heartedly. The three elements, which were strictly captured in all the PR and marketing activity, were the following:

- To clearly position Levi as the person who was going to bring Caribbean flavours to the masses, via a PR campaign that increased consumer belief in him as a creator of fabulocious sauces and food. This message was communicated consistently to trade and consumer.
- To emphasize the versatility and uniqueness of Reggae Reggae Sauce by using recipe placement online, in press, and on TV.

- To continue the sense of fun, vibrancy, and originality that Levi brought to the dinner table and barbecue.

In the second and third years, we required hard-hitting activity that raised awareness of Reggae Reggae Sauce during the strongest period of sales, the barbecue season. Our first campaign with Subway, the sandwich-store franchise, helped to drive awareness of Reggae Reggae Sauce as a marinade. We also began working with Wetherspoon's pubs, who list Levi's sauce on dishes in their menus, so that consumers can enjoy his sauces in a relaxed and carefree environment where they are more susceptible to marketing messages.

ENCOURAGE CUSTOMER/CLIENT INVOLVEMENT

People who are in a start-up situation have to act as their own brand manager.

Not every pitch can be made using a song and a guitar, but the more you can encourage consumer involvement in your brand, the better. You can facilitate this by doing the following:

- Engage with those you come into contact with, and inspire them with what you are doing, so they feel part of the brand's development.
- Understand your USP for the business and develop a USP for each service or product line as well. Your consumer needs to understand what you have on offer.

FOCUS ON MARKET POSITIONING

If you are a start-up, bringing in new consumers is of paramount importance. Very early on in the Reggae Reggae Sauce development plan, we had a conversation about fish products – and sardines in particular. Levi uses fish a lot in his cooking. If he were to launch Reggae

Reggae sardines, he would transform what could be perceived as quite a staid category into something much more exciting and fun. We would be targeting the people who had never bought sardines – until they saw Reggae Reggae sardines. Our aim would be to get them to think, 'Fantastic, I've got to try that!' and to change people's perception of sardines.

Launching a new brand is all about taking the consumer on a journey, and you are looking first at those categories that have highest consumer penetration, in order to create maximum impact. Sardines and the fish category would not have created the greatest initial impact to the largest number of consumers, so that's why we didn't move ahead with this. We didn't exclude it entirely, but we had a lot more to do before then. The link with chicken, for example, was more important for the brand, and it was our first priority.

When you go to Levi's restaurant, or any Caribbean restaurant, you'll see jerk chicken on the menu. It is the most popular dish and the one most people are aware of, so building the association between Reggae Reggae Sauce as a jerk/barbecue sauce and chicken was an important first step. Levi's sauce also tastes magical with chicken!

You have to really understand your consumer and your shopper (who may not always be the same person), so as to avoid bringing things to the table that do not have relevance. Instead, try to deliver something that is unique and will set you apart – and that adds some excitement to the category.

Frozen foods have high market penetration because they are 'centre of plate',

rather than a side dish, so Birds Eye Reggae Reggae Chicken Chargrills was a clear way to sample his flavour to a wide mainstream audience.

All your marketing and PR activity should resonate with your USP. Levi makes sure that everything we do resonates with him as a person, is fun, and can capture the unconventional nature of the brand.

When you are launching a new brand, product, or service, these are the priorities:

- Establish a clear market positioning for the brand.
- Develop marketing and PR activity that communicates a consistent USP.
- Find new ways to keep your brand, product, or service at the forefront of customers' or consumers' minds.
- Avoid lean periods, by finding ways to establish sales all year round."

CLASSIC MISTAKES THAT PEOPLE MAKE

Here are the mistakes that are commonly made by start-ups, and how to avoid them.

Loss of momentum: You have to work quickly and seize opportunities, but always remember your brand vision and ensure that you are always on track.

Paralysis by analysis: You can analyse data until the cows come home, as the sources are endless, but that will get you only so far, and only in terms of hindsight. You can see what's happened and what's been done, but this isn't going to change what the consumer thinks about your brand or make them pick up one of your bottles.

Looking backwards: Marketeers need to develop sound foresight, so they can assess what's *going* to happen. Continually taking a cautious and reactive approach by always looking at the past is a common mistake.

Giving up at the first hurdle: Never, never give up. Levi is the perfect example of someone who would never take 'no' for an answer. Understand customers' needs and motivations.

Operating without a plan: Speeding ahead without planning is never a good idea. If you don't know your destination, how will you know when you have reached it? You have to have a plan, for now and for the future, even if it's only in your own mind.

Losing control of costs: Spending lots of money without seeing any return is a disaster. Keep a close eye on the profit-and-loss statement for the brand – and make sure you thoroughly understand it.

FINDING NEW IDEAS

"It is not hard to come up with new ideas for the Levi Roots brand. Most of them are generated through working very closely with Levi himself: talking to consumers consistently at shows, through the website, and via forums. Levi's Papine Jerk Centre, run by his son Zaion, and his range of cookbooks are a constant source of inspiration. Being aware of the Caribbean community and other food suppliers is also important. We are constantly forecasting what competitors will do, having discussions with retailers, and setting up 'insight sessions' with Levi and other members of the team, to come up with new ideas and pick up on the latest trends. From the mix of sources, we test a number of ideas on loyal consumers and non-consumers, to get their reactions and to decide what to take forward.

In the short space of time since he appeared on *Dragons' Den*, Levi has launched several new sauces and a successful range of ready meals and other food products. He has had a mainstream television programme, he's published bestselling cookbooks, and he still enjoys working as a musician. Because of all these achievements, he can start to tell the story in a slightly different way. It has been a very fast journey – but it has hardly begun."

CHAPTER 6

RISKY BUSINESS

Roots of success 6:
Never be afraid to make mistakes

"We must take the current when it serves,
Or lose our ventures."

WILLIAM SHAKESPEARE

An entrepreneur is usually seen as someone who takes business risks; that is probably the most common perception people have. But business is not about taking a blind gamble. How the risks are assessed and managed before action is taken is the key to wise business decisions. Yes, an entrepreneur takes risks, but they are calculated risks, taken with 'due diligence' and confidence. No business person wants to see their hard-earned profit slip through their fingers on a whim – although most enjoy the thrill of winning the deal.

Even so, the risk sometimes doesn't pay off. You can't make the big wins unless you are willing to take a risk, and sometimes things go wrong and mistakes are made – expensive ones, too. Unforeseen factors may come into play. That is when the true nature of the entrepreneur is put to the test. Peter Jones has a saying: "There are no mistakes, only feedback." And he is right. Every mistake includes a lesson to be learned, a chance to review what went wrong, so that you can do things differently in future. If you are afraid to make mistakes, you will never make progress.

RISKS AND REALITY

Many entrepreneurs work tirelessly, taking few breaks, their minds awash with new and improved ways of running the business or closing the next deal. They are also motivated by the fear factor. It is always there, niggling away at you and asking you questions like, "What is the competition up to?" "Are sales up or down on last month?" "What is happening in this or that territory?" "Who is copying the brand?" "Is the team working well?" "Did that last promotion work?" "Where is the next opportunity?" Your mind will not rest.

The fear factor is a healthy thing – it can actually drive you on. There is never any harm in being tested and encouraged to raise your game and improve performance. If you expect the unexpected, you will be ready for it when it arrives. There tend to be five areas of business risk.

- External: Threats from your competitors or factors beyond your control, such as new technology or problems in the economy.
- Financial: Usually problems with cash flow or profitability.
- Business systems or administration: The systems you have in place for measuring performance, monitoring the money, or product delivery can let you down if they are not running efficiently.
- Regulatory: There are some rules that should not be broken, such as health and safety guidelines and HMRC and VAT requirements. You need to stay on top of these areas.
- Personal: You need the personal skills and the heart to lead, drive, and manage your team or you will have trouble getting others to deliver what you need. Most business owners will agree that this is the area that is hardest to get right, and where having a mentor can really make a big difference.

The great thing about risks is that they are also opportunities for growth and improvement. The improvement may come from the lessons you learn when you make a mistake, or it can come from a strategic decision to change the way you do things and improve your business.

Some external risks can be weighed up and disregarded, as they are not an immediate threat to your business. For example, new technological developments will usually take time to have an impact. The answer is to make sure that the equipment you buy will not quickly become obsolete. Other kinds of risk you can delegate to external experts, such as finance, health and safety, or legal advisors.

Internal risks such as administrative and operational risks need to be minimized as far as possible. At the very least you need a production schedule and a tracking system to ensure monies are paid and received on time and that you meet your contractual obligations to customers and suppliers.

If *you* are the risk to your business – perhaps you are headstrong, or lacking in experience or self-discipline – you may need to get out of your comfort zone and get some new skills that will prevent you from ruining all that you have created.

Risk is a motivator as well as a warning sign. In an ideal world, all risk would be eliminated – but, without it, entrepreneurs would be less creative, and being in business might be a lot less interesting.

> The successful entrepreneurs I know have two things in common: they thrive on challenges, and they love competition.

Being an entrepreneur is a high-adrenaline life choice. You will be tuned in to anticipating threats and dangers. The difference between the person who chooses the entrepreneurial path and the person who doesn't is likely to come down to their relationship with risk. Successful entrepreneurs I know have two things in common: they thrive on challenges, and love competition. They weigh up the options and take action. Under pressure, they show steely determination and face up to the test. Risks and challenges bring out the best in them. They may lose a few deals on the way, but they embrace those failures and dust themselves off, ready for the next venture. They are always thinking big – often *very* big. In the long run, they are richer and more famous for it.

If you are naturally risk-averse and would rather have a little nap than go into battle with your competitors, you have two main options. Either make sure that you are so far ahead of the pack that you are leading the market, rather than reacting to it, or choose a different way of making a living. I have always found that a certain level of anxiety is a healthy thing. If I am not worried, then something is not right. I welcome the worry factor because it makes me raise my game. I want to keep doing what I do in ways that are better and more innovative.

> **Don't be a firefighter. Preparation in advance is always the key to eliminating risk and increasing your chances of success. Firefighting, or being reactive, puts everyone under pressure and rarely delivers the ideal result.**

GOING IN WITH EYES WIDE SHUT

There is an element of facing up to the unknown when starting a business. My advice is always to be prepared for every forseeable eventuality. That way, even if you don't know what is going to happen, you will be ready to seize the opportunity. (Sometimes, however, it is good to be a little bit in the dark, as it means that you can be yourself because you don't know what else is expected.)

I spoke earlier about my dreams for the future and the way that *Dragons' Den* transformed my fortunes. But I have never had any doubt that something big was going to happen in my life. I just didn't know what it was going to be or when it was going to happen, so I had to make sure that I was ready all the time. I think that belief has made all the difference. If you expect the best, that is what you recognize and move towards. You make life happen as you dream it will.

In 2006 I was attending the World Food Market in east London. I wanted to liven things up a little and to bring my sauce to everyone's attention, as I'd launched it with its new name just a couple of months before. So there I was with my guitar and my 'ghetto blaster' singing a crazy song about a sauce, when suddenly I had a tap on the shoulder from a researcher from *Dragons' Den*.

They said, "Levi, we'd really like you to be on this show; we think you will be fantastic. What do you think?" I thought it must be a reality show where they would ask me to eat snakes and do other crazy things. And I thought, "No, this is not for me." But, of course, I took the business card, and the rest is history.

NOTHING VENTURED, NOTHING GAINED

I was in a fearless frame of mind on the day of my Dragon-slaying. I knew I was taking a massive personal risk. Other people had cautioned me against going on the show; they knew that my musical ambitions and my street credibility were both at stake, if the Dragons had slain me. But facing my fear of the unknown has always driven me on, and I saw this as my opportunity to reach a whole new market. I decided not to fill up my head with other people's fears, as their visions didn't fit with how I was dreaming my dream – or the ending I had seen. I didn't know what I was about to face but, whatever the outcome, I saw it as a brilliant opportunity to promote my sauce and music to the masses.

> There is a tide in the affairs of men,
> Which, taken at the flood,
> leads on to fortune;
> Omitted, all the voyage of their life
> Is bound in shallows and in miseries.
> On such a full sea are we now afloat,
> And we must take the current
> when it serves,
> Or lose our ventures.
>
> WILLIAM SHAKESPEARE, *JULIUS CAESAR*

The words of Shakespeare have influenced me a lot and, from the moment I first heard Brutus' speech in *Julius Caesar*, his words have resonated with me. "We must take the current when it serves, or lose our ventures" is such an appropriate motto for an entrepreneur. I live my life by that phrase. You need to be ready to answer the call when the time comes – and to recognize when that time is here.

From the moment you decide to set up in business for yourself, there will be moments on a daily basis where you will need to 'grasp the nettle' to make your ideas happen. All of the previous steps have been about preparation and laying the ground, but there comes a point when you must pin your colours to the mast and set sail into your newly charted waters. Hopefully you have the passion for your mission, you know where you are headed, you have your business plan and marketing plan, and you have tested the water. Now is the time to set sail.

> There is no need to set yourself adrift completely. Many people who go into business will ease into it gradually, as I did.

There is no need, however, to set yourself adrift completely. Many people starting in business for the first time will ease into it gradually, as I did. Building up the basics at the weekend or alongside your day job is a wise approach if you are a sole trader. Having a part-time income from another source can ease the way in the early stages, when cash flow may be a challenge. However, it is important to be clear where your main income and your main focus lie. Splitting your focus or having too many conflicting priorities can threaten the future outcome. You need to be committed to building your business, or it may never be more than a hobby.

THE ISSUE OF CONFIDENTIALITY

Finding someone you can talk to about your business is tricky, and it is natural to get nervous about sharing your ideas with other people. The theme of secrets and confidentiality is one of the things that people most often want to ask me about. Many people believe that they don't dare talk to anyone about their idea because someone might steal it. It is sensible to want to safeguard your idea, but keeping it to yourself is not always the most important priority.

I am not saying that you should tell the world about your idea before you have got anything off the ground, but holding on to secrets can sometimes hold you back. The chances are that no one else could manifest it in the way you would because they are not you and they are not inside your head. They haven't developed your business plan. However, deciding on the right time to share your idea is important, so, once again, it is wise to prepare your business plan and to have everything in place before you talk about your project to potential business partners. You want to be in a position to act fast once you have the right team in place to make your idea happen.

Sometimes a door of opportunity opens only once, and in order to get in you have to make a decision to trust someone. This can be a difficult decision to make. But there are always ways to deal with whatever it is that is causing you concern. The best way to minimize risk is to take advice from someone who has already trodden your path successfully.

> **❗** Once you have something tangible to sell, it
> is important to take steps to protect yourself
> legally and to make sure that you are protected
> contractually from fraud or other deception.
> See the Further Resources section for information
> on where to go for advice about contracts, non-
> disclosure agreements, and other legal measures.

Sharing the secret recipe

A few weeks after Peter Jones and Richard Farleigh became
my backers, I was travelling on a train with Eric White, one of
Peter's senior managers. We were on our way to meet the
company (AB Foods), to whom we were planning to grant
the licence to make Reggae Reggae Sauce. For the first time,
I was going to have to talk about the recipe for my sauce.

Initially I was very uneasy, so Eric and I talked through
my options. I could have held back some secret ingredients,
or I could have provided some part of the recipe myself. There
are always options. But again I had to ask myself whether
I wanted to create something potentially massive within a
quick space of time and make the most of my opportunity,
or find a way of maintaining the secrecy of the recipe?

I was back in the *Dragons' Den*, hearing the voice of
my mother reminding me that 60 per cent of something is
better than 100 per cent of nothing. I was entering the world
of big business and was facing the kind of decision that you
often have to make. I knew that I would much rather have a
business that was going to go somewhere fast than hold on
to something that was going nowhere slowly.

> Business is about building and maintaining working partnerships.

The other important lesson here is that business is often about building and maintaining working partnerships – and about each member of that partnership maintaining their side of the deal. It is in the interests of your business partners, too, to play their part by keeping your secrets. Of course, a letter of agreement or other legal document needs to be put in place, so that both sides are protected and the terms of agreement are crystal clear. But for business growth to be healthy, there has to be a marriage of commitment, not just of convenience. All of the partners who have agreements with the Reggae Reggae Group play a crucial part in the growth of the business, and we work together to make sure that the arrangements work.

NEVER UNDERESTIMATE YOUR COMPETITORS

As I said in Chapter 2, it is crucial to find out where you stand in the market. People often make the mistake of underestimating their competitors' ability to fight back. The flip side of launching a new business or becoming successful is that you draw the attention of your competitors. If you are doing something well, others will begin to copy you. It is one of the natural laws of business life.

SAFEGUARD YOUR IDEA

There are several practical steps you can take to safeguard your idea. If it is a trade name or logo, register it as a trademark with the Intellectual Property Office (IPO); if it is an invention, direct any enquiries via the Patents Office.

Patents are valid for up to 20 years at a time. Once granted, a patent will give you the right to stop other people from making, using, or selling your invention if they have not applied to you for permission. If you've invented a new product, part, or innovation; a new technique or method; or a new use for a product, think about applying for a patent. A patent is a company asset that can be bought, sold, or licensed.

Ideas, proposals, and other confidential information can be protected to some extent by asking potential business partners to sign a 'non-disclosure agreement'. If you are dealing with a reputable company that has a track record of working in your industry sector, they will be used to respecting confidential information. Their reputation depends upon it. But the true rule of thumb is to trust your gut instincts – and if necessary to ask for personal testimonials.

That is true even in a niche market such as Caribbean food because other companies are now starting to develop Caribbean versions of their sauces. The artwork on many condiments has been brightened up with Caribbean colours. The Levi Roots Reggae Reggae Foods brand and their gold and red sunshine colours have been waking up the competition.

Seeing your competitors stepping closer to your territory will keep you on your toes. It makes you constantly step up to the plate and keep thinking ahead. Everything you do as an innovator is providing those who are coming after you with innovations, too. Others are looking to you to shine the way for them. So, even though you may not realize it, what you are doing as a small niche company will be important to the big boys, because they monitor the trend that you represent and they will follow that.

The smaller fry will also be looking your way and hanging on to your coat-tails, getting as close as possible to your shining light, so that the glow reflects on them and they pick up sales as well. That is why clusters of similar types of shop tend to open in the same street or area; it is why trends occur.

The advantage of being a small company is that you are flexible; you can make decisions quickly and even change direction fast if necessary. However, once again, the most important thing is to stay true to your goals and to who you are and what you stand for. Every decision should be taken in the context of your USP and your personal strategy. The greater risk is losing sight of where you are headed and what your dream was all about.

> The advantage of being a small company is that you are flexible; you can make decisions quickly and even change direction fast if necessary.

TAKE LEGAL ADVICE TO KEEP YOURSELF PROTECTED

I have always taken business advice from lawyers. Having been in the music industry for so many years, I know how easy it is for musicians and songwriters to unknowingly give away their copyright and their future earning potential. It happens simply because they don't know how the business side of the music world works or are too inexperienced to ask for a contract or negotiate terms.

It doesn't matter whether you are in the music business, the food business, manufacturing, the beauty industry, fashion, or any other industry – at some point, when a transaction takes place and money changes hands, you will enter into a business agreement. It makes sense to take legal advice to make sure that you are doing things the right way – and to protect yourself in advance in case anything should go wrong. Business basics, such as setting terms of business, taking on board the basics of employment law, setting up contracts of employment, or understanding whether you need indemnity insurance, can be made so much simpler if a legal expert is involved.

Taking legal advice is not about being over-cautious, but about thinking ahead and reducing the risk to yourself, your home, and your business. See Andrew Subramaniam's advice on finance (see page 236) and Teja Picton Howell's guidance on the value of legal advice (see page 183) for more detail – and see the Further Resources section for helpful general information, too.

RESPECT REGULATIONS

Make sure that you operate within the official regulations and guidelines for your industry and trade. Believe me, there will always be some of these somewhere. Import duty, export duty, VAT, copyright, licensing laws, professional accreditation… the list goes on. It is your responsibility to find out what you need to know. You may not agree with the guidelines, and the rules may seem time-consuming or even annoying, but it is not worth risking your business future by breaking the law.

The food industry is one of the most tightly regulated in the business world. Agents from the Health and Safety Executive visit frequently, unexpectedly, and often at very busy times. It is very important for my team to stay on their toes and to make sure that everything is spotlessly clean and stored properly, and that the food stock is checked daily.

YOU WILL ALWAYS LEARN MORE FROM YOUR MISTAKES

My experiences have shown me that, even in your darkest hour, there is light to be found, and there are new roads to be taken. Although making mistakes is not enjoyable, my advice is always to take your setbacks on the chin and look at the lessons you can learn from your experience. These lessons can always be found if you seek them out.

Nothing in business is certain, and the unpredictable will happen, so at some point even the best-run business will come under pressure. There is no point in blaming anyone else if that happens. If you are the owner, the buck always stops with you.

One of my earliest business ventures was a fledgling clothing empire called the High Fashion Boutique. I set it up in a lockup belonging to my brother in Brixton, in 1990. I was fresh out of prison, with little hope of getting a job, but that didn't bother me. While I was in prison, Theresa, the arts liaison volunteer, had helped me to see that I didn't have to repeat my past mistakes. She encouraged me to develop the 'true me'. I couldn't wait to get out there and put the past behind me. I was full of self-belief and raring to go. All I had was an open lockup and an empty shop, a chamois leather and a spray can of Mr Sheen. I told my brother that I would turn it into a business overnight. In fact, it took me a week.

My good friend Lloyd Coxsone had the lockup next door. We had toured together and recorded my 'Poor Man's Story' song. He laughed when he saw me down there each day, just chatting away to people and cleaning the place up. When I told him that I was going to run a shop, he said, "How are you going to do that? How are you going to get the money? You've just come out of prison and nobody trusts you. All you've got is a 'shami' and a Mr Sheen." It is still a joke between us today.

I wasn't sure how I was going to make it happen, but I just headed back there each day and focused on making the place as sharp as possible. I had a sense that everything would fall into place. And it did – in the form of a wonderful lady called Sister Dan. She came to see me one day with a whole range of linen suits. She had imported them from Africa and, even though linen was very much in fashion, she was having trouble selling them.

It was the moment that I'd been preparing for. I said, "I'll take them off you on a sale-or-return basis" – and so I did, selling them at a mark-up of 50 per cent above what she had bought them for. It was the same business model that I had learned in the record business.

So, I had my premises, and I had my stock. I also had my customer base because I had spent so much time chatting to the community and getting to know people again that everyone came to see what I had been getting up to. I put fabric on the ceiling to give the place a warmer feel. It looked great, and I worked hard to make it very welcoming. People came to catch up with me as much as to try the clothes. It reinforced what I had already discovered – that, first and foremost, people buy from people. Because they like to feel good about themselves, they want to be associated with a feel-good brand.

> First and foremost, people buy from people. Everyone likes to belong. Because they like to feel good about themselves, they want to be associated with a feel-good brand.

As the suits sold, so I had some cash to play with, and this became my start-up capital. I next decided to invest in some American-style T-shirts from the United States. I asked my customers what styles they liked, and I took pre-orders from my friends, so that by the time I ordered the clothing I was already confident that the range would sell.

I travelled out to the States and bought the T-shirts myself. Clothes were incredibly cheap in America compared with in the UK. I knew my market, and I knew the mark-up that the market would take. The stock sold quickly. Sister Dan soon had her seed fund back – and I was in business. Levi Roots had arrived.

But few things in business are totally straightforward, and I was about to learn a very big business lesson. I had no contractual agreement with my brother. He had the rental agreement with the landlord, and I paid rent to my brother, but we hadn't formalized the arrangement. He decided very suddenly that he wanted the lockup back and that he would take on the shop – stock and all. There was nothing to say that I owned the stock. On paper it was his because it was on his premises. It was my word against his. We fell out over that very badly for a time.

But we both learned great lessons as a result. I learned how important it is to take legal advice and to keep my interests protected by having a proper agreement in place; he learned that there is more to running a successful business than hustling. People buy from people – not just because they like the goods. The customer base fell away, and the shop closed soon afterwards.

Connections are important

Years later, the valuable lesson I learned while running the High Fashion Boutique played an important role in my changing fortunes. As soon as Peter Jones and Richard Farleigh offered to invest in my business, I wanted the best lawyer I could find to represent me in my negotiations with them. I gave my music lawyer, Henry Ellis, a call. I trusted Henry – he had been looking after me in the music industry for a long time. I told him that I wanted to make sure my interests would be protected if I won the investment I was looking for. He knew exactly who I needed to talk to. He had been to university with Teja Picton Howell – a corporate lawyer, and the perfect person to help me.

The very first day we met, Teja told me, "I am going to show you how to make money with the least effort possible!" Ha! I've never forgotten it – and it wasn't just an idle boast. What he meant was that my own time spent on the business was just as much an investment as the money that Peter Jones and Richard Farleigh were about to invest. I should work hard, to make sure that I always got the best return on my time invested in the business. If you construct a good business deal and protect your interests, you can share with other people the burdens of the business as well as the profits – and your rewards will come, in the context of the long-term plan.

Teja negotiated the details of the investment into my company, and put together a shareholders' agreement with Peter Jones and Richard Farleigh before I signed away 40 per cent of my company. They were very surprised I had got a hard-hitting corporate lawyer to represent me.

Teja has been looking after the interests of Levi Roots and the Roots Reggae Reggae companies ever since. Henry Ellis did me a big favour in introducing me to him. And that is another important lesson – don't take unnecessary risks when seeking advice. Always begin by asking those you know and trust for recommendations.

> I am going to show you how to make money with the least effort possible!
>
> TEJA PICTON HOWELL

WHAT IS A PRE-EMPTION RIGHT?

Richard Farleigh is a speculative investor. It was the profits rather than the brand that were his long-term interest, so naturally there would come a moment when he would want to sell his shares in Roots Reggae Reggae Sauce Ltd for a profit. That moment came just 18 months after he invested in my brand. A pre-emption right gives the shareholders in the company the right of first refusal should one of the other shareholders decide to sell their shares at any time. When Richard Farleigh decided to sell, the pre-emption rights that Teja had insisted went into the investment agreement between me, Peter Jones, and Richard Farleigh meant that Richard was contractually bound to offer his shares to me first. And even though that cost me a fair amount of money, it meant that I was able to prevent the shares being sold to anyone else, and maintain control of my company and my brand. That was crucial. Without that deal in place, Richard would have been free to sell his shares to the highest bidder – and who knows who Peter Jones and I would have on board as a third business partner now. Teja's deal protected my interests from day one.

SUCCESS WILL HAPPEN –
ONE STEP AT A TIME

Managing risk and moving on from your mistakes are important skills to learn in the business battlefield because they take you ever closer to your goals. Success will happen, one step at a time, but you need to keep your spirits buoyant. Your attitude is important, too. The biggest risk you will need to manage – is you.

> The biggest risk you will need to manage – is you.

A lot of people have to learn to be confident, and it can take years of experience and practice. Fears and anxiety are linked to the unknown. Compensating for anxiety by being over-confident, arrogant, or defensive can push potential business partners away, but a lack of confidence will undermine their belief in what you have to offer.

Confidence is often gained by first practising what you like doing. My way of dealing with this is to focus on the thing that I like most about what I have to do. There is always something that will keep me there: the positive outcome, for example. You also have to be true to yourself. That is the only way to take away the risk of going into something new or unprepared. If you are the kind of person who will always wait until you have everything in place, the moment for the idea may pass you by.

In the early days, when I was faced with a series of refusals from the banks and other investors, I didn't take it personally, and I made sure that they never made me falter. I knew that all I needed was a single 'yes' then everything else I had lined up would fall into place, like dominoes.

> Hanging on to the memory of previous failures is like carting around unnecessary baggage. Learn the lesson and then let it go.

If you have had a setback, make sure you cast off your disappointment quickly – because the people you talk to at your next meeting won't want to know about the ten failures you have had before. They will trust you for what you put in front of them. Any kind of negative thinking on your part will affect your state of mind and be reflected in your attitude, which could influence the outcome.

No one can afford to take business setbacks personally. Business is business, and success builds future success. If a positive person stands in front of potential customers or investors and says, "This is who I am, and this is what I have to offer," they will reduce the risk of being turned down and move closer to the 'yes' that is needed to make things happen.

HOW TO CREATE YOUR OWN LUCK IN BUSINESS

Teja Picton Howell is an essential part of the Roots Reggae Reggae Group of companies. I trust him to anticipate what issues we will meet as we take the business forward and especially what might go wrong, or what could come up that I haven't thought about. He will assess the risks facing the business generally and when we face a new transaction. He will forewarn me of things and try to negotiate the risks away or to ring-fence and minimize them commercially and contractually. He will also be there to advise me on my new ventures. He has done hundreds of deals and has the experience to know how, why, and when things can go wrong – and the best ways to make sure things go right.

Sometimes his role is just to take the flack when negotiations get tough or heated, and to diffuse problems, to make sure that the deal stays on course. Usually impeccably polite, he can be direct and tough when necessary. Nothing and no one fazes him. When you are aiming for the big time, you need someone like Teja on board.

Don't worry about knowing all the answers before you go to see a lawyer because, if you have a good rapport with them and they know their stuff, they will tell you what you need to know. If they don't – and if you don't feel your questions have been answered – they are not the right business associate for you.
• Go in asking questions.

- *Do a 'rapport check'.*
- *Make sure that they are listening to you.*
- *Check that what you are hearing is appropriate for your needs.*
- *Ensure that they understand your vision.*
- *Make sure that what they are suggesting is in your long-term interest.*

Teja Picton Howell, corporate lawyer

"People keep telling me how lucky Levi is to have been so successful over the past few years – but his success is not down to luck. It is down to vision and sheer hard graft. Levi never stops working. Not everyone recognizes the years of dedication that went into getting his business off the ground. He has always been a trier, and really is the hardest-working guy I know. His commitment doesn't relate only to his business; for example, during most weeks he will visit a number of schools, speaking to pupils about entrepreneurship and the importance of self-belief. Every business decision he makes is in the context of a clear long-term vision.

BE SERIOUS ABOUT WHAT YOU DO

What first impressed me about Levi was the seriousness with which he was approaching his business. This is a man who, knowing that he was about to meet with five corporate investors (on *Dragons' Den*), made sure that he would have a lawyer to represent him when he won the investment. He didn't go into the Den unprepared. He was already working to a very carefully thought-out business plan – and his commitment and his passion were unquestionable.

Levi lives brands and marketing. He has an intuitive understanding of how to communicate his products to people. He is also a great listener, has an excellent memory, and absorbs absolutely everything. This is just as well because when his business started to take off Levi had to take the fast track into a world that was new to him. It is a world of business jargon – liquidity ratios, cash flow projections, valuations, internal rates of return – that even those with decades of corporate experience don't always fully understand (although they would never admit it). In meetings Levi may say little, but he listens hard and misses nothing. He has an acute ability to focus on the salient points that others may miss (often the issues that make the real difference between the deal working or not working, or how profitable the deal will be), which means that when he does speak, people listen.

Listen to and evaluate good advice

There is a view that being a good negotiator is just about being tough – about dominating the negotiations or making the most noise. However, it is often the quieter, more considered party (the one who observes everything and misses nothing) who is in the stronger position.

Levi has been careful to surround himself with good people who can advise him on the big strategic decisions and can also deal with the small details. When he makes decisions he takes account of that advice. This doesn't mean that he always agrees with every recommendation, but when he doesn't agree, it's for good, considered reasons. It comes down partly to having natural good judgement and partly to thinking things through. He will always consider things, rather than making a knee-jerk response. Levi has always made his own decisions in life, and in business he takes responsibility for the decision-making process, but he is also an effective and empowering delegator who allows other members of his team to make decisions in their own areas of responsibility.

Have confidence in your team

Levi has managed to grow his business very quickly by putting the right people in place and giving them the authority to get on with it. He shows them the direction for the business, but without micro-managing every decision. He has confidence in his people, and the confidence to let them get on and do their jobs and work towards the shared goal.

Not everyone is able to delegate effectively. The skill does not necessarily come easily to self-starters who are ambitious, driven, and determined. Many entrepreneurs have to work hard to learn how to delegate, but until they do their businesses will not grow. One of the biggest mistakes you can make in business is to try to control every aspect of a business yourself in the mistaken belief that you are leading it, when all you are really doing is focusing on the administration.

Levi is very clear about the big picture. He knows and shows us daily where the business is going. He recognizes his own skills, strengths, and weaknesses and makes sure that his team has the right skills to complement his own. His time needs to be as free as possible, to allow him to focus on what he is best at: promoting and developing the Levi Roots and Reggae Reggae brands.

Build relationships based on trust

To build a lasting, profitable business you have to 'walk in a straight line'. Successful business comes from building good business relationships based on trust, agreement, and reliability. Levi's business is based on good products and a strong brand, and when a deal is agreed we have to make sure that the legal relationship with the other party is carefully defined in a legal document to avoid any problems in the future.

Lawyers use the phrase 'a meeting of the minds' (consensus ad idem) to describe one of the requirements of a legal contract. Deals work best when both parties know exactly what is expected of them and what they will get back in return, and then both parties do what they have agreed to do and what is expected of them. Push someone too hard to go beyond what they are willing to give you, or get them into a negotiation that they don't really understand, and the deal will probably break. Then, however strong your legal documents, it is all likely to end in tears.

That doesn't mean that you should take your eye off protecting your own best interests. One of the reasons that the business relationship between Levi and Peter Jones has worked so well is that they recognize one another's strengths, and you don't achieve that success without having a very strong focus on how to maximize profits. Peter invested into Reggae Reggae Sauce because he could see how it could make him money, but he also saw what value he could bring to the business over and above his financial investment. Levi and Peter have a very good, clear working relationship. They bring out the entrepreneurial best in one another – because it is a business relationship based on respect, trust, and mutual benefit.

When people ask me how my business relationship with Levi works, I tell them that Levi does the funk, and I do the legals! Corporate lawyers all the time see business opportunities that show great potential, and I have been in business long enough to know that the potential is not always achieved. But in Levi's case the potential is being fulfilled, because he has unshakeable belief in his business and unerring commitment. That's what gave me the confidence to back him, as a client.

WHAT TO LOOK FOR WHEN SEEKING LEGAL ADVICE

I think, as a broad generalization, there are two types of lawyers: processing lawyers, who offer technical skills, and advisory or more proactive lawyers. The first category includes lawyers who will drive a process and do as they are told. For example, they will set up a company for you or prepare a shareholders' agreement for you. The vast majority of lawyers will do tasks such as this adequately. But then there is the second category: the lawyers who take a far more hands-on approach, who are committed to helping the client and driving the business forward. These are the people who get stuck in, taking an active commercial interest in your business, and who want to understand how it works and how you make your profits. This type of lawyer helps you to understand the commercial risks and challenges you face, finds solutions, and helps you to identify opportunities that may not always be obvious.

Lawyers, through their training, can be very risk-adverse. One of their main roles is to help you to identify the risks your business faces. However, the lawyer who sees all the risks, but can offer no solutions, won't help you take your business very far.

A good lawyer can bring much vicarious experience to the table, because he or she is involved in many people's businesses and therefore sees a lot of things that work and a lot of things that go wrong. That experience can be very valuable to you. When you start your own business, you may not have put together a lot of other transactions or business structures, whereas a good corporate advisor with broad experience can bring you the benefit of their own experience and their knowledge of the mistakes and successes that other businesses have made.

Protecting the client's interests

A lawyer's job is to look at the way your business agreement is structured, and to make sure that things work in your best interests. That's not at any cost, of course. A lawyer shouldn't assist a client to do something illegal or dishonest – or, for that matter, immoral – but should be there to promote your interests.

When choosing the professional you want to work with (whether a lawyer, accountant, banker, or anyone else critical to your business), you have to ask yourself the following questions: Can I work with this person? Do I trust them? Do I feel comfortable with the advice they are giving me? Will I have to check everything they do? Or can I rely on them to get on with their job to the best of their ability – and in the best interests of my business?

A good advisor is one who will listen, who makes sure they understand what the client is trying to achieve then presents the options, and who actually gives positive, active advice rather than just using their technical skills to draft a document.

A question of cost

One of the greatest challenges for a small business or a start-up business is the question of cost, especially if you have very limited funding. Inevitably there are choices to be made, such as whether you spend the money on marketing or on drawing up a document that outlines your terms of business. The reality is that lawyers' services are expensive, and every pound spent on legal fees can be a pound less spent on something such as marketing or recruiting a new person needed to help drive the business forward. Spending on a lawyer is like any other spending – there has to be a return on the investment.

Very often, your legal expenses are about protecting your business against risk – for example, making sure that you have well-drafted employment contracts and personnel policies to reduce your risks of an employee claim, or setting out clear standard terms of business so that your legal liability to customers is limited and so you can effectively enforce payment from a difficult customer. Any lawyer will tell you that prevention of a problem is always better than cure. You can spend as much as you like on legal fees to try to address

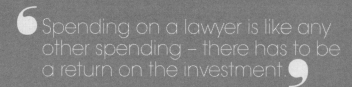

6 Spending on a lawyer is like any other spending – there has to be a return on the investment. 9

every possible risk facing your business. But that's not commercially realistic.

As with any other business expense, you have to make sure that you are getting the best return for your investment. This will involve judgement and some compromises. You have to make assessments not only of the different risks to your business but also of the consequences if something does go wrong.

Part of the craft of the lawyer should be to recognize that their client has limited financial resources and so to help prioritize and allocate spending on legal advice in a way that brings the most benefit to the business.

THE BENEFITS OF LEGAL REPRESENTATION

When you first meet with a lawyer (or with any kind of advisor), ask yourself:

• Are they giving you advice in their best interests or in your best interests?
• Is this someone I can trust?
• Is this someone who will back me?
• What kind of return will I get on my investment?

However, you also need to be realistic about how much time they will be able to give you for the budget you have available.

Levi's business

Roots Reggae Reggae Sauce Ltd and Levi Roots Reggae Reggae Foods Ltd are businesses based on legal relationships. It's about granting other companies the right to use the Levi Roots and Reggae Reggae brands, and protecting those brands. We're giving licensees the legal right to use the brand for a period of time, for a specific purpose, within a particular market. We need to be very clear what the legal rights being granted to each licensee are. Those rights are regulated within a legal document (usually a licence agreement), negotiated, and then entered into between Levi's companies and the licensee.

There are many different kinds of business, and a specific kind of contract or style of agreement will be needed according to what your business is offering. Some businesses are legally simpler than others (for example, you don't negotiate and sign a legal contract when you buy something from a shop). But those businesses dealing with intangible rights (such as brands, trademarks, and other intellectual property, secret recipes or processes, or services) will probably need carefully prepared legal agreements. This is the case whether you use standard 'terms of business' for all of your customers, or whether you negotiate a 'bespoke' agreement for each new transaction.

Creating a win-win situation

One of the greatest benefits of engaging a good corporate lawyer is to try to ensure that the deal works commercially as well as legally. Levi could choose to take the approach whereby his company pushes as hard as possible for the biggest payment and the most onerous terms, while making sure that he holds all the cards. However, we like to create business agreements that are win–win. There should always be a benefit to both parties. For example, when we give someone the right to produce and market one of Levi's products, we try to make sure that the licence is granted for a period of time that is long enough for the licensee to gain a return on their investment. We want our partners to make a long-term commitment and a real investment, and so we have to ensure that there will be a good long-term return for them if they do so. Levi is also very loyal to the people he does business with. He prefers to build long-term business relationships that will build value in his business, rather than look for just short-term gains.

The popular media often portrays aggression as an effective tool in business. In my experience, taking an overly aggressive stance is rarely effective. If you can't see how the other guy is going to make a profit out of the deal, it is unlikely to be a good deal. You might have the tightest legal documents in the world, but where a deal is unbalanced it is likely to 'break' or go wrong. And when it goes wrong, both sides will probably end up as the losers. The best deals work on a mutuality of interest.

If you do a deal and someone signs that deal willingly, then, in my experience, even if the deal goes against them in the long run, they will honour the terms of the deal, because they entered into it willingly. But if they feel that they were pushed into something that they didn't want to do or didn't understand, then the deal will break, and they will find ways of seeking revenge or undermining the deal, or will try to make their money back from you in other ways.

Asking the hard questions

In business there are some hard decisions to be made, and companies may start negotiation with directly opposing interests. At the simplest level this may be: "I want to pay as little as possible; you want me to pay as much as possible." But the differences have to be resolved and in such a way that it enables the parties to maintain a good working commercial relationship.

Sometimes it can be better for the really tough

negotiations to be done by a legal advisor who is slightly detached from the business, so that the ongoing business relationship between the people directly involved in that business is not soured by the tough negotiations. To some extent, the role of the lawyer is to ask the hard questions, to go into the difficult meetings, to weather the arguments, so that the main parties to the deal can carry on working together without any tensions from the negotiations affecting their relationship.

Reaching consensus

One of the most important roles of the lawyers in any deal is to try to ensure that there is a 'meeting of the minds', so that both sides have a clear (and the same) understanding of the deal they are doing, what is required of them, and what they can expect in return. The lawyers do this by asking the questions that the parties may not have considered themselves, and by making sure that the legal agreements correctly reflect the intentions of the parties and are in accordance with the principles of the relevant laws."

> ! The fundamental basis of a contract under English law is offer, acceptance, consideration ie value (value given by each of the parties to the other) and *consensus ad idem* (a meeting of minds).

The mistakes business people make aren't usually legal mistakes; they make commercial mistakes that then have legal implications. The legal input is just one of the tools used to achieve the commercial outcome. There are several recommendations that I would make to help ensure that the risks to your business are minimized:

Have very clear objectives: Know what you want to achieve. Constantly ask yourself, "Is the decision I am about to make going to take me closer to my objective or further away from it?" Every question should provide a clear answer once the context of that question and the objectives are clear. I have seen Levi pass over commercial opportunities even though they might deliver considerable short-term profit because they don't fit in with his USP or his long-term objectives. He makes every decision on the basis of building long-term value for the brand.

Cash is king: It's a cliché, but still true. Make sure that your business model is cash-positive and protects your cash flow, and therefore that your legal model protects cash flow. Even a profitable business with weak cash flow will run into problems. Your commercial agreements (such as how quickly your customers pay and how quickly you pay your suppliers) should leave you with enough cash to run the business. Next, make sure that your legal contracts (or your terms of business with customers) reflect and protect those commercial arrangements. The legal model must follow the commercial model, not the other way around.

Make sure that you have carefully prepared and tested cash flow projections: A model for the business that shows how much cash you expect to receive and how much cash you expect to pay out over the months ahead – and that you monitor cash flow projections on a daily basis. Good cash flow modelling will show how much initial capital you will need to get the business off the ground. It should also enable you to predict cash flow problems before they hit, and help you to manage your business in a way that ensures you do not run out of money. (See Chapter 8 for more about finance.)

> The legal model must follow the business model – not the other way around.

Understand your risks: Business is about taking entrepreneurial risks, but the biggest threat to the commercial success of a business is not assessing and managing those risks in advance. That doesn't mean that you shouldn't take risks. But make sure that you take them only after having made an assessment of the risks the business faces – and the possible consequences of those risks should they go against you. You can then take the appropriate steps to protect your business or manage those risks.

Communicate clearly what you are willing to offer and what you require in return, and make sure that your agreement is documented: You may not always require a full-blown, legally drawn-up contract. In many cases a clear exchange of emails will be sufficient – but make sure that there is a clear understanding and agreement between you and the other parties involved. Recording things in writing not only protects you if you need to pursue any legal remedy, but also ensures that both parties are doing the same deal. Disagreements don't necessarily arise because of bad faith – deals more usually go wrong through misunderstandings as to what each person expected from the other. Make sure from the outset that you reach a real meeting of the minds.

Always walk in a straight line: Levi often quotes Shakespeare: "To thine own self be true." I put this another way: "Always walk in a straight line." Be clear with people about what you are doing and your reasons for doing it, and go straight to where you want to get to. Don't beat around the bush or try to mislead. Levi "walks in a straight line" in business, which has enabled him to do some big deals with some very large companies. My advice is to do business only with other people who also walk in a straight line.

CHAPTER 7

THE TEAM – WHO'S IN, WHO'S OUT

Roots of success 7: Surround yourself with like-minded people

"OneLove"

LEVI ROOTS

More and more people have an ambition to go into business these days. Programmes such as *Dragons' Den, The Apprentice,* and others are helping people to see that being successful in business is both possible and something to aspire to. Business people have become the new generation of role models. Successful businesses are seen giving back to the community, new start-ups are creating employment, and, of course, the material success that comes with success can provide comfort with all the trimmings. At the end of the day that is what being in business is all about.

Being in business can also offer opportunities and better prospects to people who haven't gone to university or to those who find it hard to conform within a traditional job. It is important that people who have had a tough start in life can see that others from the same background have been able to make their own way – in spite of setbacks. It offers them hope. They will realize that they have the chance to succeed and make positive choices about their future. There were no obvious business role models from my culture who I could identify with when I was growing up. I would have liked to have seen some black Levi Rootses already out there blazing a trail.

What few of the business entertainment programmes show is how important it is to have a good team around you and how much more can be achieved if everyone is pulling together. If you surround yourself with like-minded people, you are more likely to reach your goal because everyone will be pulling in the same direction, with shared enthusiasm. They will also learn from and inspire each other.

> There is no better place to learn and be inspired than as part of a team in the workplace.

LEARNING BY OBSERVING

The people who shape us help to make us. Everyone needs someone to look up to and learn from. When we are children that person is often a parent or other relative, or a teacher. As an adult it is more likely to be someone who you respect for being very good at what they do. As I said in Chapter 4, I am a great believer in mentors – in using them and in being one – and if your mentor is also your manager or your leader, then so much the better. That is a great combination. The best way to learn is by observing, then doing, under a watchful eye.

I have often learned new skills by watching how other people do things, as well as by reading, studying, and listening. As a young boy I learned to cook by watching my grandmother while she sang as she worked in the kitchen, joyfully preparing traditional Jamaican food. Later I learned much of what I know about music from some of the biggest reggae names of the 1970s and 1980s.

My earliest true role model was Bob Marley. *Natty Dread* was the first of his albums to be released on Island Records, and it was the first one I listened to. It opened my mind to what *I* wanted: to try to find *my* path in life, and to want to be like this Rasta man, singing his amazing songs. I used to watch these talented people on stage and think to myself, "One day I want to be up there with them because I know that music is going to be central to my life." And that is eventually what I managed to make happen.

I try to surround myself with like-minded people, and I set myself goals to make sure that I achieve that. In that way it is always possible to learn from the best. Although such people may not be formally part of your business team, they can nevertheless influence the way you think and your business behaviour.

> I try to surround myself with like-minded people, and I set myself goals to make sure that I achieve that. In that way it is always possible to meet and learn from the best.

WHO'S COOKING WITH YOU?

Another benefit of surrounding yourself with like-minded people is that everything goes more smoothly when there is a shared vision. You may be the one who is setting the pace and who has the vision, but setting targets and putting the process in place to deliver on those targets involves everyone who has responsibility for delivering the different elements of what you do.

When you think back to your SWOT (see page 46), ask yourself what skills you need to balance your weaknesses. What kind of people do you want to have on board? It is not just a matter of whether you like them, but whether they are competent to do the job they do and whether they will gel with everyone else on the team. When your business is small you can't afford to 'carry' people. Make use of a three-month trial period, and don't be afraid to take a tough decision if you think you have made the wrong choices. (But take advice. Employment law is full of rules and regulations.)

MANAGE YOUR BUSINESS OR IT WILL MANAGE YOU

Those who are successful will often look sharp, unruffled, without a hair out of place. Rather like a duck moving smoothly in water, all is calm on the surface. But surface appearances don't tell the whole story. Take a closer look underwater, and you'll see all the paddling that goes into that duck's seemingly effortless glide. Similarly, you will know how hard *you* are paddling, but you don't want anyone else to see all the hard work that is going on beneath. It is important to find your rhythm while you are paddling and to stay upright, knowing and being aware of all that is going on around you.

The way I deal with pressure is to welcome it. Pressure means that things are happening. If you try to avoid pressure, you are also walking away from success. You can't have one without the other. The keys to managing pressure are:

Honest communication: Communicate with everyone involved in the situation.

Delegation: Don't try to do everything yourself.

Preparation: Break everything down into manageable chunks and tasks.

Organization: Be systematic in your approach, and stay on top of things. Time is on your side if you schedule it in advance.

Hard work: There is no short cut to success. Reducing pressure takes hard work and experience, which can only be gained over time.

Fitness: Get fit for success by looking after your body, as well as your mind, with plenty of sleep, a good diet, and exercise.

LEAD FROM THE FRONT

If you want to run a business, you have to be able to lead. That's it – there is no other option. It would be nice to be able to say that anyone can do it, but it's just not true. If you are extremely shy or you don't feel comfortable representing yourself, you will need to get someone else to step into those leadership shoes for you. Leadership ability is an essential to inspire others to follow you. You need to have an air of authority for others to put their trust in your judgement, so that your team pulls together and everyone wants to achieve the same goal. An investor will want to be reassured that the money they provide for your business is being protected by you, the strong character.

People in their twenties and thirties will not yet know what they are capable of as leaders or managers. Confidence grows with time, courage, and experience. You grow, and everything you do offers a learning experience. It is all about what you are willing and able to learn – and how you shape up once you begin. I tell people the following:

- You will never know the true extent of all your talents until you have to learn new things.
- You will always have to try.
- Get used to making decisions by learning to prioritize.
- At the end of the day, it is your business and you are accountable.
- Keep taking the vitamins – your mind has got to be sharp.

Keep in touch with the grassroots level

Those at the top need to keep in touch with what is really going on in their business – at the point where the customers are buying your products or using your service. I have tried to set things up within my company so that I always get to hear early on if something isn't right. If my sauce is too hot or too spicy, I want people to tell *me*, so I can put it right.

I have a single email address that is directed to one person who then filters everything and liaises where necessary with my PR team who run the diary. If there is a problem with something, they will forward it to me, or to the most relevant person on the team. Even if it is an automated message, we always try to respond.

The speed of communication when responding to comments is very important. If you delay responding to something – whether it's from someone who's happy or someone who is unhappy – everybody becomes unhappy.

That can do damage because people don't know that as an individual you are incredibly busy. If they've written to you and made a complaint, it is important for the company to be set up in a way that can deal with that situation. It's always about priorities – and, for me, the public is the priority because they are the ones who keep on buying my products.

Distribution priorities

Effective distribution is vital. You can have the best goods in the world and everyone may want them, but if you can't deliver them where they are needed, you might as well not bother. A distributor will always want to know about supply and demand. They will want to know that what you're supplying is good – but more importantly that you can supply in regular, large-enough quantities to meet the demand.

If you're delivering to a supermarket, then they will get the distribution arranged for you. Alternatively, you will have to arrange your own distribution. It could be something you decide to do yourself initially – you won't need a fleet of lorries at this stage, and you would get feedback direct from the customers. It depends on the logistics and where your priorities lie. If you have a stack of products to get out of the door, you'll probably need to hire someone in to stuff the envelopes and get them to the post office because your time will be better spent elsewhere.

DELEGATION IS THE KEY TO SUCCESS

You need to be good at respecting other people's professionalism. For example, there may be occasions when Teja, my legal advisor, will make decisions on my behalf. They may not be the same decisions that I would have made. But if you delegate, or if you appoint someone to take responsibility, then provided they use their judgement to make an informed decision, you have to back them on that decision. An entrepreneur has to trust and feel comfortable with the people they rely upon.

As a business owner, you need to paint a clear picture of what you want people to do. If you communicate explicitly where the business is going, and what part your colleagues play in taking it forward, then how they achieve that is to a great extent up to them.

There will be times when you do have the wrong person in the wrong place. Then it is a case of grasping the nettle and taking the hard decision, letting them know, moving them to another position, or moving them out of the business.

THE STORY OF TWO PAPINE CENTRES

There is always more than one reason for running a business, and it is never only about making a profit. Back in the 1980s I had a venture in Brixton called the Papine Pool Centre. I wanted to create a meeting place that was a little like Papine in Kingston, Jamaica, where Papine market is an exciting hub of vibrant people and noise and music and laughter. The music is never far away. The original Papine is like a terminus and the hub of all things that are happening. It's a meeting place where all the buses come and go, and the market is alive with colour and food smells and people chatting.

When I went back to Jamaica for the first time since I had said goodbye to my wonderful grandmother, Miriam, I realized how much a part of me that country was and how much I missed it. My first Papine wasn't mainly about making a profit; it was about recreating a little piece of my beloved Jamaica, right here in my back yard. It was about the community, and it survived only because they gave it their support. More often than not, I was subsidizing it out of my own pocket. Unfortunately, I had some trouble on the premises (which is how I ended up in prison). But in spite of the problems, the business was always about the people first.

The second Papine is a very different story. The Papine Jerk Centre is my Rasta'rant and is my way of paying back to our community. It is an extension of what my sauce is all about: me and my children and the importance of family. I talk about family a lot – it means everything to me.

When my kids were younger we would all gather around the kitchen table and cook together. We still do the same thing now, but quite often it happens in the cafe. All my commercial recipes begin in Papine Jerk. It keeps me in touch with what people really want – and it is all about family.

When I first launched my Reggae Reggae Sauce in the days before *Dragons' Den*, my vision was all about building a family business – and Papine Jerk Centre is exactly that. We provide school meals to local schools, and we have also helped kids who have got into trouble to turn their lives around – and it has worked.

Not all my business advisors understand my motivation to build Papine. It doesn't sit naturally alongside the big corporate plans for the Levi Roots Reggae Reggae Foods business. But in my mind it is a perfect fit – and it is an important part of what I am about. It has a different kind of business model to the rest of my companies. Perhaps the profit margins are not as sharp as they are for the sauce, and we may appear a bit more relaxed to passers-by. But cooking meals for several hundred children five days a week is a busy challenge, so my team run a pretty tight ship.

> There is always more than one reason for running a business, and it is never only about making a profit.

KEEPING A BALANCE

People ask me when I am going to stop and take a break, and whether I have had a little celebration to mark how far my company has come in the past few years. I do think this is a good idea for some – people should reward themselves if they need to. I rarely do so, however, because it's not really me. Although I was over the moon to gain Peter's and Richard's backing in January 2007, I didn't celebrate. I hadn't yet begun! My opportunity is here and now, and I need to keep up the momentum. Chilling and relaxing are not what is needed just now. I am the one who has to keep driving the train, because I want it to take me as far along the track as it can be powered to go. I'm so focused that I always have my eye on work and what is happening in the business. In my mind I still have a long way to go to fulfil my dreams and ambitions.

Anyone who is self-employed will have the same dilemma: how to keep their business growing and not let family and loved ones feel neglected at the same time. In the past three years, I have written three cookbooks, released an album, and developed more than 20 new Reggae Reggae food products. I have done a lot of promos with supermarkets up and down the country, taking my guitar and singing songs, and it has all paid off – the sales have gone through the roof.

The tricky part is to bring everyone else along with you, at the pace at which you are going. So much of what is happening is in my mind and not on paper. It is not until the results start to show that those around you really begin to understand what it is all about – then they want to hop aboard that train with you.

I am a bit of a taskmaster at work – I do drive people hard to get the best out of them. But I reward them for their hard work, too. A leader has to lead from the front; it is all about showing strength of character and being the last person standing. It may mean that you have to crack the whip a bit, too, because it is your business and there is a lot at stake if it doesn't work – and no one to blame but yourself. It is too soon for me to take my foot off the throttle. I don't want the next opportunity to appear while I am off sunning myself somewhere – I want to be around to "take the current when it serves".

KEEPING IT IN THE FAMILY

I think trust is very important in business relationships. I am lucky to be working with people who are excellent at what they do. Once you have the right people in place, you need to let them get on with it. Otherwise there will be mass confusion.

I know my own strengths, but I also know where the skills gap lies, and I am very happy to take advice from those who are more experienced than me in those areas. My core skill is in sales and marketing – enthusing people, so that they love the sauce and the other products as much as I do and want to be part of the whole Levi Roots business and music journey. It is a feel-good brand, and I want everyone who comes into contact with it to feel good, too.

As my son Zaion explains on page 213, we keep the business in the family. We are fortunate that we all get along so well and that there are enough of us to be able to build a team of people with the skills we need to succeed.

Zaion is in a unique position. Not all sons will have his opportunity, but his situation and experience will resonate with others who are starting out in business. If it were a long-established family business, the next generation would be learning from the legacy of the first generation. Children from business dynasties know from birth what their heritage will be, and they are prepared for that. But it's more as if Zaion and I are climbing that ladder at the same time.

A STRONG TEAM MAKES A SUCCESSFUL BUSINESS

Anyone who is ambitious in business will know they need to remain diligent and learn as they go along. It is vital to learn how to work as part of a team and to realize that everything you learn contributes to the decisions you make for the future good of the business.

My eldest son, Zaion, is typical of many who will be reading this book and entering into running their own business for the first time. Zaion runs our Papine Jerk Centre in Battersea, London, with the family team and some backup from me. It is a big responsibility because of its close association with the Levi Roots brand. Five years ago, we were just a normal family from Brixton, with ambitious plans for a fledgling business. So, coping with the pressure of having a father who has been thrown into the public eye, while becoming the manager of a successful restaurant, with no previous experience, is quite a challenge. Like me, Zaion has had to learn how to run a business fast, by being dropped in at the deep end. As a family, we have all had to put on our business clothes very quickly.

I work closely with Zaion as his mentor, offering him the benefit of my experience. So he has my expertise wrapped up with Nadia Jones' and Peter Jones'! It is natural to have fears and anxieties alongside your dreams and *ambitions but it is realizing that you do not have to cope with them unsupported that makes the difference.*

Zaion Graham – manager, Papine Jerk Centre

"You need to be very hard-working and energetic to make it in the food business. There is always something to occupy your mind, and at Papine Jerk Centre we have had to learn a lot, quite fast. When we first discussed the idea of my running the family restaurant, I found the idea daunting. But it was also an exciting prospect, and I relished the challenge. I took some time to take stock, to decide whether it was something that I really wanted to do – and had the skills to do. I felt that it was important to take a look at myself first, to decide what I had to do and whether I could do it, before I took up the idea. Once I had made up my mind, I just took the bull by the horns.

Having my father as my mentor probably makes my situation a little different to most people's because I have been learning from him all my life. There are so many skills that Levi has taught me growing up, in cooking as well as in business. People tell me that I am a lot like Levi, and I think that is true. Although I am very much my own person, with my own ideas, I do try to learn as much as I can from him. He has been a great inspiration to me throughout my life, and he has done really well for himself. I can only try to follow in his footsteps. I've been training for this my whole life, really, and I learned the tools of my trade from a very good teacher.

TURNING AN ENTHUSIASM INTO A BUSINESS

I don't think you'll ever find a Jamaican person who can't cook. It's part of everyday life and is instilled into you from a very young age. I have been cooking, and have always loved to cook, since childhood. I love experimenting with different tastes and flavours, and putting things together. My early enthusiasm for the restaurant was definitely more about the cooking than the desire to be a business owner. But realizing that we could create a business that combined the success of the sauce with recipe development meant that both concepts progressed hand in hand.

Running a business, and having to focus on supply and demand and cash flow, is definitely quite different from making and selling a product for fun. One of the important things we did from day one was to set up a system to monitor the core elements of the business. These included keeping track of our stock and sales, the book-keeping, the accounts, and other aspects of the business. They are all as important as each other, and we needed to ensure we could string them together nicely.

When we first started selling the sauce we used to make about 64 bottles a week in our kitchen at home. Everyone in the family was involved. We used to peel all the peppers and onions, our eyes would be streaming, and we would be up to our elbows in ingredients. It was a big step up to get to what we are doing now, but a good transition. Now, everything we do is about giving the brand a certain reputation. We stay focused on the quality of our products and keeping the quality of our food to a high standard.

The great push from *Dragons' Den* put us many steps ahead of where we were at the time, but we always had a business plan for doing our own little thing. We always believed that we would take the sauce to a wider audience, though never in my wildest dreams did I think it would do what it has done today. Knowing that every time we open our doors we are representing Levi and the brand, as well as ourselves, could obviously be seen as a pressure, but I try not to look at it that way – because the alternative would be less pressure with less success. I am sure that none of us would want that, so the pressure is welcome. Instead I deal with it by remaining very focused.

ZAION'S KEYS TO STAYING FOCUSED UNDER PRESSURE

- My main tool for managing pressure is preparation. If I have prepared in advance to the right level, then when it comes down to the actual work, there is not as much pressure because I am fully prepared. That's my key tool.
- I try to find ways to save time. I pay attention to detail. There are always a few things that will save you time here or there – that will also reduce the pressure in the long run.
- I work with a like-minded team. We play to people's skills in different areas, but we also work together well. That means no one is left doing more or less than another person. We gel together and help each other out.
- I try to do things systematically dealing with one thing at a time. A kitchen is a really fast-moving, high-intensity environment. There are pots that are hot, fires going all over the place, and steam everywhere. So you've got to keep cool and stay in control under pressure.

Running a business and motivating people are very different skills to creating a fantastic recipe. However, I have a slight advantage at the Papine Jerk Centre because everyone on my team is family and, of course, Levi oversees all of us. Perhaps that wouldn't work for everyone, but we're lucky that our family is close-knit. Dealing with problems is not really a problem for that reason, because we pull together. I am a team leader and maybe I'll have the final say, but we all take responsibility for decision-making and we do things as a team.

The catering industry is in my blood from both sides of the family, because my mum is a great cook as well. I string together influences from both my father and my mother, and just have a great time with the ideas really. I enjoy getting inspiration from other cultures and learning about new flavours that go together well. I think that's what cooking is all about: your own taste, your own flavour; creating recipes to make food just the way you like it. In cooking, as in all businesses, it's about finding a way to make your mark."

THE USP FOR THE PAPINE JERK CENTRE

We are a Caribbean restaurant, serving Caribbean food. Our USP is linked to Levi Roots's USP, "put some music in your food". When you come to Papine you won't just get great music – you'll have a great meal, really good service, and you may meet Levi, too.

There is something else that we try to offer as well. We play a role in our local community, and that's really quite special. We cater for the local school, and the kids really enjoy the meals. When I see those meals going out, I feel really good, because I know they're getting fresh, hot, authentic, healthy home cooking. The kids are so bright-eyed and intelligent, and providing the fuel for them to take it all in and learn more is great for me. I feel really proud when they come across and request some more.

ZAION'S TOP TIPS
FOR MANAGING A SUCCESSFUL TEAM

- It is important to have a USP, so that everyone shares the same vision.
- Your team is just as important as your product. If you have a good team around you, who are like-minded and hard-working, you can't go wrong.
- You need to be resilient, because business is tough and you will face challenges. It will be easier to keep going if you are doing something that you are passionate about and is dear to you – that will influence those around you, too.
- Keep your finances up to date – every day. Keeping your books and your book-keeping straight is just as important as keeping track of your stock and your sales. Knowing your incomings and your outgoings is an important side of business, and it needs to be done accurately. We take 10 or 15 minutes at the end of each day to sit down and go through what we did the day before. Doing it promptly, every day, will save you time. If you leave it until the end of the week, it will take even longer and it also becomes hard to catch.
- You can never learn too much. You will always pick up different things and you will always learn as you go along.
- Make the most of any opportunity. I am Levi's son, but I am also my own person, and I'm trying to make my own way in business. It's good to have a helping hand and a big push, but after that it is up to the individual person to make the most of any opportunity and to find their own management style.

CHAPTER 8

ON THE
MONEY

Roots of success 8:
Focus on finance

> *"Money won't create success, the freedom
> to make it will."*

NELSON MANDELA

I am in business to make money. It is not the only reason, and it is not my only motivator; but making money is what keeps me focused and keeps my foot on the business accelerator. When life gives you a chance, you don't throw it away by putting on the brakes while you are still gaining speed. But I don't pretend to be a financial expert, and my company is only a few years old. I couldn't have grown the Reggae Reggae companies as fast or as profitably without the benefit of excellent financial advice – from both my investors and my accountant.

> Making money is what keeps me focused and keeps my foot on the business accelerator.

Putting together your financial forecasts and setting a budget for your business plan before you get started is vital for future success. But it is not the same as monitoring that budget from month to month, controlling cash flow on a daily basis, or knowing when and how to pay the tax-man and the VAT-man. Too many businesses fail because business owners have a blind spot about financial management. They don't seek, or can't get, the advice they need at an early-enough stage, or they try to go it alone when the going gets tough.

Therefore this chapter is about basic money matters and how to develop strong working relationships with your financial advisors. It is always worth paying for financial guidance from someone you trust – to make sure that you set your business up in the right way – and then checking that you have systems in place to keep your budget under control and manage that all-important cash flow.

This is a short chapter, because not many people find reading about money as interesting as making it, but it is an important one, so now is not the time to close the book or wander off to the kitchen for a little snack. Instead, have your business plan at the ready – the budgeting that you did earlier and the targets that you have set will chart your progress towards finding your business treasure.

IT'S TIME TO GET REAL

Finance is a common weak spot for business owners. It is all too easy to get so caught up in the enjoyment of what you like doing that you lose track of your spending and whether you are making a profit. Not everyone will have the patience for spreadsheets and the nitty-gritty of monthly or weekly (sometime even daily) profit and loss accounts or balance sheets or reconciling bank statements, nor will everyone have budgeting or financial experience. I know I haven't. I have been a mortgage advisor, but that was more to do with selling a range of products than calculating a balance sheet.

WHERE'S THE PROFIT COMING FROM?

Your accountant is an important member of the crew on your business ship and needs to have a clear picture of your long-term destination. He or she has charted similar waters many times in other businesses and knows how to plan the most successful route to your riches. An accountant will also know how to read the warning signs as you enter the calm before a damaging storm. But beware – you need to seek advice early and then listen up. By the time you are in stormy waters it may be too late to get the help you need, and your business vessel could be one of the many that hit the rocks and sink without a trace.

Your projected sales, cashflow, and profit will all be in the business plan that you created on day one. Don't let it gather dust in a file somewhere; make sure you use it as a working document, because there are two important aspects to managing your finances.

Your annual accounts are retrospective. They have to be submitted to HMRC with your annual tax return. They show how you have done during the last financial year but they don't reveal how you are doing at this minute – or what kind of cash you might need to cover your expenses in three months' time to keep the business afloat.

You will need to produce management accounts, recording how your business is doing on a monthly, weekly or even a daily basis as it happens. The more up to date you keep your management accounts, the clearer picture you will have of the health of your business at any time. You will probably also want to do sales forecasts and cash flow projections, to show you how many sales you have to do, and how quickly you need to get paid, to keep the business solvent and profitable. The heart of business management happens here – keeping an eye on the pennies each and every day.

Common pitfalls for young businesses include:

- Not working out or understanding the costs of the business, or how many sales needed to cover those costs.
- Not working out the working capital requirements and cash flow model for the business: how much cash does your business need to stay afloat.
- Not managing the cash to make sure there is enough to cover liabilities like VAT, corporation tax or rent.
- Expanding too quickly, building up expenses until the business has the sales and cash flow to pay for them.
- Relying too much on one customer.
- Unfavourable credit terms.
- Bad debt and slow payers.
- Over-production or over-commitment.
- Taking on the wrong business partners

Always look ahead and make sure you are managing your cash flow. The secret of good cash flow and profitability often lies in the details, such as negotiating extended credit terms with your suppliers while securing quick payment from your customers. Tight inventory management – making sure there is minimal wastage – is important, too. Your accountant will know the tricks of the trade and will be happy to share their knowledge with you. Remember: if you are not making a profit, you don't have a business – you have an expensive hobby.

> At the end of the day, the financial decisions are yours to make. Those around you can advise and help you, but as the business owner you need to make your own decisions, so, of course, the mistakes and the profits are yours, too!

FINANCIAL JARGON – IT'S ONLY BUSINESS LYRICS

A lot of people think they don't understand business or finance because of all the jargon that surrounds it. Well don't let a new set of lyrics stop you getting to know the song. Listen up and tune in, and you will soon figure out what people are talking about. Much of it is common sense, though there may seem to be a bewilderment of meaningless words to begin with. If your accountant is blinding you with science, ask for a translation. If you are in a high level meeting, you might want to stay quiet and make a note of the terms you don't know. You can always look things up afterwards and make sure you are savvier next time around.

The basic rules of making money are pretty simple: you need to earn money faster than you are spending it; so make sure you include in your costs absolutely *everything* you will need to spend on the business; calculate how many units you need to sell and at what price before you will make a profit; and then sell, sell, sell like crazy, to make sure you keep costs under control. After you have put aside what is due for tax and VAT, the rest is potentially your profit.

Of course, in practice it is a little more complicated than that – especially once your business gets larger. But by then you will be able to afford more of your accountant's time, and they can take some of the weight off your shoulders.

For those of you who haven't bought that dictionary of business terms just yet, here is my quick rundown of the meaning of the most common business terms:

Business plan

This is your recipe for success, your road map to riches (see page 89). The business plan sets out your business objectives and strategies, and maps out all your projected sales, costs, profits, capital requirement and cash flow to show how to get there. Topped off with your USP – your Unique Selling Point – it is a commercial description of the vision you have in your head and a description of the passion you have in your heart. Everything else flows from your business plan. Don't start your business without it!

Cash flow

There is a business saying 'cash is king'. Cash flow is not the same as profitability. Sometimes even an unprofitable business can have good cash flow (hiding the fact that the business is making losses) and a profitable but poorly-managed business can have poor cash flow. Cash flow is how quickly you collect the cash in and how quickly you have to pay it out again. If you have to pay your suppliers 'with order' but you are giving your customers 30 days credit, your cash flow will be weak and you will need a lot of working capital to fund the business. When you start employing other people you will have to pay them weekly or monthly, without fail, even before they have generated any income. That all needs cash, and you need to manage it carefully.

Managing your cash flow is one of the most important parts of your business. Make sure you keep it under control:
• Set up a credit control system to chase payments.
• Have a schedule so that you deliver on time. If you don't, you won't get paid on time.

- Put your customer first and make it easy for them to buy your products and do business with you. Are you the king of business who can take orders over the telephone, email, or internet? Where is the buzz around your brand?
- Maintain good management accounts so you can keep an eye on your cash flow, to avoid a crisis or prevent you from taking orders you can't handle. Poor cash flow and overtrading (expanding too fast) are common reasons for business failure.
- Create a supplier management system, and keep an eye on supplier costs.

Cash flow projection

You should try and work out how much cash your business will need by carefully preparing cash flow projections. The best way to do this is by building a financial model for your business on a computer spreadsheet. This lets you test the effect of different scenarios on your cash flow. If your business is growing fast, it will eat up a lot of cash if you have to pay suppliers and employees, or invest in new equipment, before you get paid by your customers. By projecting the outcomes you can measure the amount of working capital you will need and make decisions about whether you can fund this from existing cash flow or whether you will need additional investment or borrowings to fund the growth.

Working capital

Most businesses need an amount of cash in the business to keep running. This is called the working capital. You can work out how much is required from your cash flow projections.

The tighter you run your business and manage cash flow, the less working capital you will need, and so your return on investment (profits) will be proportionately higher. You can fund the working capital in different ways, for example by the money you originally introduced to start up the business, or by retaining profits within the business, getting a bank loan or overdraft facility, or finding people willing to invest in your business in return for owning some of the shares.

Solvency

There are two tests for solvency. If your business is generating enough cash to pay all of its liabilities as they fall due, then your business is 'liquid' or 'solvent'. Solvency is also where the value of all of the assets of the business exceeds all of its liabilities. However, if the business can't pay all of its liabilities as they fall due, or all of its total liabilities exceed the value of all of its assets, then the business is 'insolvent'. A business can be insolvent even if when is profitable, but an insolvent business, unless it can become solvent, is likely to fail sooner or later.

Overdraft

An overdraft is a flexible facility from a bank that allows you to borrow money for your business, pay it back again as you receive cash, and then borrow the money again as and when needed. An overdraft for a small business is usually repayable 'on demand', which means that the bank can ask you to repay the debt, or stop you drawing out any more money, at any time. The advantage of an overdraft is that you only pay interest on the money that you actually use (although the bank may charge you an annual arrangement fee). An overdraft can be 'unsecured' or 'secured'. A secured overdraft is where the bank takes a charge, or a debenture, over the assets of your business, which puts them first in line in getting paid before the other creditors. Very often if a limited company has an overdraft the bank will ask the directors or shareholders to give personal guarantees; that is, to be personally liable if the company doesn't pay. Very often a personal guarantee will also be secured, for example by second charge over the director or shareholder's house. This means that it is ultimately you, rather than the bank, taking the risk on the loan.

Accounts

This usually refers to the annual accounts of the business that are prepared retrospectively, after the end of a financial year. That's useful for seeing how you did, but doesn't tell you how you're doing now or how your business will be doing in the future. You should also produce 'management accounts' that help you manage the business by giving you a more up-to-date picture. The management accounts will also be used as a basis in preparing the annual accounts.

Balance sheet

The balance sheet forms part of the accounts and is a snapshot of the business on a particular date. It doesn't tell you whether the business is trading profitably or not. It shows all of the assets and liabilities of the business (at least in accounting terms) and whether the business has surplus assets (called 'shareholders funds' or 'equity') or if the liabilities of the business are more than the assets (in which case the business is insolvent).

Fixed assets

These are the assets owned by the business, such as machinery, buildings or intellectual property rights, used in the business. The fixed assets are usually shown on a balance sheet at the actual cost of acquiring them, and then 'written down' or 'depreciated' over the expected life of the assets. The amount of the depreciation each year is shown in the profit-and-loss account, and so reduces the profits of the business, but then affect the value of the fixed assets shown on the balance sheet at the end of the year.

Current assets and liabilities

Current assets are the trading assets of the business, such as cash, money receivable from customers (book debts), stock available for sale and work in progress (i.e. work has been carried out but has not yet been completed). Current liabilities are the liabilities of the company payable within the next 12 months, such as debts due to suppliers, outstanding tax, bank overdrafts, etc. The current assets and current liabilities are netted off on a balance sheet to show the net current assets. If current liabilities are more than the current assets, instead the balance sheet will show net current liabilities.

Long-term liabilities

The long-term liabilities of a business will usually be long-term loans.

Net assets

The net assets of the business (also called 'equity' or 'shareholders funds') are what are left after all the liabilities have been deducted from all the assets.

Profit-and-loss account

The profit-and-loss account (sometimes abbreviated to 'P & L') shows how the business has traded over a specific period of time. It shows all the income and expenses from the business, and what is leftover is the profit for that period (or the loss if the expenses exceed the income). Some of the figures on the P & L will be actual, such as the value of goods sold and invoiced or expenses paid, and some will be income or expenses (for example depreciation) recognised in the accounts even if they haven't been actually received or incurred in order to give a true and fair view of the overall profitability of the business.

Turnover

Turnover (or gross turnover) of the business (also sometimes called 'revenue' or 'income', or more casually the 'top line') is the total amount of sales (net of VAT) for the period shown in the profit-and-loss account.

Cost of sales

These are the costs directly attributed to producing each product sold or service supplied. For example, when I sold a bottle of my home-made Reggae Reggae Sauce I had to buy the bottle, the ingredients and the label. Those were my cost of sales.

Gross profit

The gross profit is the difference between the total turnover of the business and the total cost of sales. For example, if your sales sell are £1 million and annual cost of sales are £700,000, the gross profit for that period is £300,000, (a gross profit margin of 30%). If you work out your gross profit per unit sale, you can work out how many units you have to sell to break even. For example, if my turnover (ie sale price) per bottle of Reggae Reggae Sauce was £1 and my costs of sale for that bottle were 70p, my gross profit per bottle would be 30p. If you work out that all your direct costs and overhead costs (see below) were £30,000 a year, I would know that I had to sell at least 100,000 bottles a year just to break even. If I sold any less my business would be unprofitable, and if I sell more then my business should go into profit.

Direct costs

These include all costs that are directly attributed to producing and selling a product, such as the costs of the employees working on the production line, and the cost of delivering that product to the customer.

Overheads

These are the costs of the business that have to be paid irrespective of how many products you produce or services you sell. For example, you have to pay the rent for a factory whether you produce and sell a million units a year or don't sell any at all.

Profit, or net profit

Profit (also called net income, net earnings, or 'the bottom line') is what you are left with at the end of the year after you have added up all the turnover and deducted all your expenses. However, the figure shown in the P & L might only be the 'paper profit' (on which you may have to pay tax) and not necessarily the increase in the amount of cash you have had in your bank account. For example, you may have produced stock which goes into the P & L but has not yet been sold and turned into cash; or you may have sold products that have not yet been paid for. Some of the expenses on your P & L, such as depreciation, may not have cost you actual cash that year. Always remember that profits are not the same as cash flow, and it can be quite painful to pay tax on your profits before you have received the cash. You can calculate your net profit margin by dividing the turnover for a period by the net profits. For example, if my net profit was £1,500 on a turnover of £10,000 my net profit margin would be 15%.

Economies of scale

This is where the more you produce, the cheaper each unit will be, usually because you are spreading the overhead costs over a larger number of units or because you can afford to purchase bigger, more efficient machinery or get better discounts from your suppliers. However, diseconomies of scale can also apply, where the bigger you get the more you have to invest. For example, had I purchased some £10,000 worth of bottling machinery so that I wouldn't have to make the sauce at home in my kitchen, the first bottled sauce I produced on the new machinery would have cost me £10,000!

Return on investment

This is calculated by dividing the amount of investment by the amount of annual profits made (or dividends received). An investor investing £25,000 into a company and receiving dividends for £3,750 a year would be receiving a return on investment of 15%. However, the return on investment can also be calculated by reference to the profits made on the sale or repayment of that investment. An investor who invests £25,000 into shares and sells a year later for £50,000 has made a return on investment of 100%. An investor will be looking for a good return on investment.

Budget

This little word covers a multiple of things. There are all kinds and sizes of budget, but for now let's keep it simple. Your budget is your planned spending and part of your cash flow management. It is the amount of money you have estimated that you need in order to run your company over the next six months to a year. It will take into account all your costs and other requirements and will be allocated to all the different areas of your business. So, for example, you might have separate budgets for research and development; production; marketing; sales and administration.

Your budget should take into account the overheads in each of these areas and include your sales forecasts and any new product launches.

Your budget is your map of the big financial picture. It works hand in hand with your daily cash flow, so that you make sure you are spending within your budget at all times. If your turnover is less than you had projected, then you may have to reduce your budgets (or on the other hand you may decide to increase your budget on marketing to try and build up your turnover). The point is, a carefully worked out budget and monitoring of your cash flow will enable you to make informed decisions.

Every time you go over-budget in any area, you eat into your profits and mess up your cash flow. So you need to be disciplined and ensure everyone else in your team understands the plan and knows how important it is, too.

KEEP IT SIMPLE

There are all kinds of resources available that will offer advice on how to manage your cash flow. Some of these are listed on pages 275–279. Here is some basic advice:
- Decide your pricing scale and your rates of discounts, based on the projections in your business plan – and keep to them.
- If you are asked for a quote in advance, include all charges, such as delivery, postage, and VAT (if applicable).
- If you are offering a service rather than selling goods, take account of all of your time.
- Keep track of all your invoices and spending on a day-to-day or weekly basis.
- Note when you are due to be paid, and chase up promptly and politely.
- Keep all your receipts (and write on them what they were for).
- Make a note of all the money you put in and take out of the company.

Set up a system that works for you, and stick to it. Make managing your cash flow a regular habit – the action that signs off your working day. That way it won't be a major task, and you will always know exactly where you are in your financial picture.

WHEN THINGS GO WRONG

Even the most successful business people will tell you stories of business collapse, where things went wrong and other near misses. They also agree on these basic guidelines:

- If you see an iceberg ahead, remember that you are closer to trouble than you think. Speak to your accountant and your bank manager, so that a potential crisis can be avoided and managed in advance.
- Don't panic. Those around you need you to keep a cool head, as they will be looking to you for guidance.
- Keep communicating. Your family and your team need to know what is going on, so that they understand how it might affect them.
- Get to know your bank manager and your financial advisor. Befriend them and take their advice. If they like your plan, they will also like you and be more willing to back you.

- Take action. Financial problems won't go away if you ignore them. The last thing you need is a poor credit rating and a bad reputation among your suppliers or with the bank.
- Be flexible. A good business plan will include a financial model that will enable you to feed in different assumptions as to sales, pricing, etc. so that you can test different scenarios to see how they might affect cash flow or profitability. Plan afresh, and keep to the plan, but keep reviewing it.
- Refresh your passion for what you do. If the joy has gone out of your work, decide how the next tide of development will re-motivate you or whether the current has served its purpose and you no longer want to be in its flow.
- Knuckle down to work. The best way to get out of trouble is by applying yourself and working hard – very hard if necessary.

Some of the most successful business people in the world have made it and lost it all several times over. As Peter Jones would say, "There is no failure – only feedback." We can all dust ourselves off after making our mistakes and take on board the lessons learned, so we reach our new goals more quickly and efficiently than before.

MAKING EVERYTHING ADD UP

Andrew Subramaniam has been my accountant for several years and is a vital part of my management team. A lot of the nitty-gritty of what Andrew does will always remain a mystery to me, but he knows the rules of finance like I know Scotch Bonnet peppers.

There is no point in trying to become an expert in tax and VAT when you have a trained professional to ask for advice. He is my short cut to spotting any financial weak spots in the cash flow and finding the best ways to make my money work within the business.

Like Teja, my lawyer, Andrew helps me to minimize risks and to maximize money-making opportunities and long-term profits. I always listen to him and I trust what he has to say, because he talks financial sense. However, I don't take all of his advice all of the time. Sometimes I may choose to sacrifice short-term profit for the goal of polishing a longer-term gem that is important to me. But he understands that – and we always keep the lines of communication open.

Andrew Subramaniam, chartered accountant
"Levi's story can never be said to be 'rags to riches' because he always dresses so well. Rags have never come into it! But there is no doubt that his background has been challenging, and involving

financial hardship. In spite of rocketing to business stardom in recent years, he knows that his success has been long and hard-won, which is reflected in his work ethic and his determination to build the Reggae Reggae Group into a sound and profitable company that has longevity.

Anyone who works in a creative industry is always going to have their own ideas, so when it comes to taking financial advice it can be hard for people to conform to tried-and-tested methods. Levi is not like that at all. He certainly is creative – to the core – but he has great respect for, and appreciation of, other people's skills. He has an astute mind and, while he knows what he's good at, he also knows what he needs to learn from others to make his plans work. That's a very big business lesson to learn. He has an astute mind. Perhaps it's because he has made it slightly later in life. He knows

where he comes from, and he doesn't want to forget that.

His awareness of his community shows in his dedication to the Papine Jerk Centre in Battersea. He is a successful business man, running a community cafe in the middle of a housing estate. Some people on his advisory team may ask why he is doing it. What does it have to do with building 'brand Levi'? But he enjoys cooking for the children in the school opposite, and creating the menus, giving back to his community. He is saying, "This is who I am and where I came from." The next minute he is off to meet the Prime Minister to discuss a business initiative.

Part of my role is to help Levi decide how to allocate his time. As hard as it is for me to say – and for him to do – I constantly tell him, 'If you're going to develop the business, you've got to restrict your charity appearances to maybe one week a month, as opposed to one every other day. Focus on your promotions and maximizing your business opportunities, because you just don't have time to do everything.' He doesn't necessarily see it that way. We have running battles about it, but I wouldn't be doing my job if I weren't giving him the right advice.

WHAT DOES AN ACCOUNTANT DO?

An accountant, like a business advisor, lawyer, or bank manager, has a useful role to play in assessing whether your business idea and your plan are financially viable. They can also help you to set up your company in a way that will be tax- and cost-efficient. An accountant will focus on how you can get maximum financial return by looking at how you manage and spread your costs.

Many people going into business for the first time, especially if they are very creative, have the mistaken perception that, whatever their idea is, it is going to be a success. You see this error all the time on programmes such as *Dragons' Den*. It never ceases to amaze me how inventive people can be with their ideas; however in reality 99.9 per cent of creative ideas won't support a profitable business.

A common mistake is that the majority of people assume they should be setting up a limited company from day one – and they probably want to start off by renting premises as well. But that can be costly if you are earning less than, say, £30,000 a year. The accountancy fees alone would increase significantly because there are additional start-up costs involved and there would need to be a set of formal accounts prepared for filing at Companies House.

I tend to suggest that new business owners set up as a sole trader and operate in this way for six months to a year to see how things develop. I look at their financial affairs and help them to consider what they might earn in that time. After the first year, once the business is better established, we can review earnings and look at incorporating the business into a company that is appropriate for their needs, looking forwards.

It is possible to run a payroll and operate as a sole trader in just the same way as you would if you were incorporated as a limited company or limited liability partnership. Insurance can be taken out to cover general liabilities such as accidents in the workplace.

From day one you should look at the structure of the company and know your financial objectives. If you don't get the structure right from day one, you'll spend half the time when you should be growing the business playing 'catch up' because you don't know where you are with the financials. People come to me with grand ideas, and part of my job is to think about the practicalities and make the ideas more realistic.

Even though the individual, operating as a sole trader or a small company, might feel daunted by the cost of an accountant, a good one is an important investment. They think for you in a way you probably haven't the experience to think for yourself.

HOW TO FIND AN ACCOUNTANT

I am a chartered accountant and have been in the accountancy profession for 20 years. Most of my clients come from personal recommendations. When you are looking for an accountant for the first time, go to someone whose business you respect and ask who they would recommend.

If you need specialist knowledge, try looking in the trade journals associated with your industry or on the accountancy institutes' websites. Look out for the following qualifications after the accountant's name as an indication that they are chartered: FCA, ACA, CA, FCCA, ACCA.

Some clients treat me like an extension of their business, while others may only need my input once a year to submit a tax return. They may be concerned with keeping the fees as low as possible, or perhaps their business model is a very simple one, so their affairs don't warrant a lot of advice. Equally, however, there are clients who prefer me to be their main contact with everyone, from HMRC to the bank manager and their suppliers. We offer a complete book-keeping and payroll service and we prepare and submit VAT returns as well.

HOW CAN AN ACCOUNTANT HELP YOUR BUSINESS?

An accountant can help a business either at the basic level of preparing accounts and submitting annual tax returns, or at a more strategic level helping a business owner to assess where they want to get to and how they will get there. The more closely involved the accountant is, the better their ability to wave the red flag if the company is heading into trouble – or to give the 'thumbs up' when the company is at a point where strategic business expansion might be on the cards.

In an ideal world, a client would come to me with their completed business plan and say, 'I want to launch a business that will be earning me X amount per year in five years' time. Here is my plan. How can you help to get me there?' In reality, that rarely happens. Business owners need to have some idea of how to run their business. They need to be ready to take responsibility for their actions and their livelihood, then they can let their accountant worry about the intricacies of the things they haven't thought about."

> **If you apply to the bank for a loan or an overdraft, be aware that there are likely to be financial covenants within the agreement. For example, the bank may be willing to lend you the money – but under the terms of the agreement they may be able to request all the money back, in one hit, unless you make a profit within 18 months. Always read the small print, and always negotiate the terms of the agreement.**

ANDREW'S TOP TIPS FOR WORKING WITH YOUR ACCOUNTANT

- Talk to your accountant if you're in any doubt about anything. Literally anything.
- Ask for advice *before* you have agreed a deal – not afterwards. By then it is often too late.
- Negotiate reasonable terms.
- Keep your accountant informed of your plans.
- Work with someone you trust, so they can help you to build your business.
- Respect the advice your accountant gives you, and have confidence in what they advise and what they do for you.

THE MOST COMMON REASONS FOR BUSINESS FAILURE

Two of the most common reasons for business failure are not to do with money, but with lack of trust and lack of communication. You've got to build a relationship with an accountant that works both ways. They can only help if you communicate with them. The classic reasons for business failure are:

- Lack of trust (in your accountant)
- Lack of communication
- Over-complicating the structure of the company
- Overtrading
- Poor cash management

Entrepreneurs by their very nature want to expand and grow the business. But sometimes this can happen too fast, which is called 'overtrading' – transacting more business than the amount of capital in the business can sustain. For example, if you are running one shop, you need to allow time for the business to become established before you open the second. As Levi says, you need to grow a strong business in your local market before you start focusing on moving your trade abroad. I advise people to get one project at a time firmly established before they move on to the next one.

I would rather my clients came to me first, to discuss the numbers and to see what is possible, than have to help them to retrieve a situation retrospectively. I can help them to drill down into the detail. If one retail outlet is doing well and another is not, you have to look at why – right down to the items on offer. What is selling? What isn't? What is earning its shelf space or menu space, and what should be dropped, re-priced, or changed? You have to go down to the core of it.

It's all very well doing work on behalf of your client, but at the end of the day your client is their own person. They may not always want to do what you advise.

PLAN AHEAD

A lot of people find the administrative side of running a business a bit of a bind. I often remind clients that if they keep their accounts up to date on a regular basis they will save money on their accountant's fees. People like hearing that! Pay attention to the detail of setting up your business. Get the structure in place on day one – and set up systems to keep your finances up to date. (Your accountant can help with this, too.) Those things alone will increase your chances of success.

Planning ahead for one year to 18 months on a rolling basis is usually enough – but keep an eye on your financial figures month on month.

You need to watch your budgeted costs and projected revenue vs your actual costs and revenue.

- Forecast is long-term (between one and five years).
- Budget is monthly or quarterly.
- Cash flow is daily or weekly.

KNOW YOUR EXIT STRATEGY

An accountant can also help you to plan your 'exit strategy'. All business owners should have an idea of how long they want to run the company for and whether they will want to sell at some point. This has an impact on the way the company is set up in the first place: for example, whether the set-up monies should be treated as a loan, so you can take them back at a certain time and whether you treat them as share capital – which will attract investors."

ANDREW'S TOP TIPS FOR MINDING THE MONEY

- Look ahead.
- Watch the small print on loan agreements. Be very wary about offering your home as financial security.
- Keep your financial forecasts simple and realistic – and up to date.
- Make sure your income is based on something concrete. Know where (and when) the money will come from.
- Try to have contracts lined up before you start your business. Always negotiate.
- Know what expenses are going to come up, and know how much it is going to cost to run the company over the next six months. Be wary of hidden costs.
- Include all costs in your business plan, such as rent, premises costs, operational costs, starting costs, professional fees, interest on your overdraft, contingency for sickness, and so on – everything should be in there.
- Negotiate favourable payment terms with suppliers.
- Do your homework. For example, do credit searches on anyone who will be paying you money.
- Avoid giving your customers or clients credit (instead, get a percentage upfront).
- Get advice on whether to register for VAT.
- Make sure your company systems and stock management are efficient.
- Turn your financial management into a habit, not a chore.
- Work with your accountant, communicate regularly, and take their advice.

CHAPTER 9

KNOW YOUR VALUE

Roots of success 9:
Stay true to your values

"Don't gain the world and lose your soul,
Wisdom is better than silver and gold."

BOB MARLEY

Why do I see personal values as one of the ten roots of success? Because if you do not know yourself or you lack respect for yourself or your work, you will find it hard to be consistent in your business dealings and decision-making. If you do not know your own value, others will find it hard to respect you – and your business or your reputation may suffer. I put a lot of stock in loyalty and constancy in my business dealings. Like the success of a company, such things are hard-won and develop over time.

What are your values? What matters to you in your working relationships and in the nature of your product or service? If you revisit the SWOT analysis that you created for yourself on page 44, how many of the points you listed were also a reflection of your values? Your personal values will influence every area of your business.

ALWAYS RESPECT YOURSELF AND OTHERS

There is a Rasta saying: "You have to acquire self-respect first in order to show it to others." I have no time for people who do not honour themselves or show respect for others. These two virtues are determined not by the distribution of wealth or health, but by the nature of the person.

> Most people will judge you first according to your material wealth. After that they will dig deeper, to see if you've got the soul and if you've got the right attitude.

People tend to judge each other initially by their material success. The signs of wealth are also the signs of achievement and a mark of personal reputation. To acquire them, we must first attain and show honour and respect for ourselves. You could say that this will also help your cash flow because once again you have to show yourself ready: ready to become wealthy. With wealth comes responsibility. You have to honour other people, especially your customers – it's a mark of success. Your customer is king. Your customer is always right. If you respect your customers, you will look after them. If you give them what they want, they will come back for more – and you will both receive more of what you want.

These days people look out for expensive brands. The belief is that 'what you see is what you get'. Although this is not entirely true, unfortunately it is what the world has become. That is the reality, especially in the world of business. So we have to have that self-respect, and show an outer glow of confidence and self-assurance, if we want people to open up to us.

> You have to acquire self-respect first in order to show it to others.

Three of us were walking through Knightsbridge one day, fresh from a meeting and in our suits. A tramp was sitting on the ground and he called out, "Please man, help me out," or something like that. I'm not sure the others even heard or saw him, but I happened to stop, dig into my pocket, and give him a handful of coins. He looked up to say thank you and suddenly recognized me: "You're that guy off the telly with the sauce. You're Levi Roots." I was taken aback that he knew me. It was a small moment, but to me it shows that, no matter how wealthy we are, it is the heart of the person that we are all looking for. When I showed respect and honour to him, I got it back from him. It really drove home to me that you've always got to be yourself and show what you're about. We will probably both remember that moment.

UNDERSTAND THE VALUE OF YOUR BUSINESS, YOUR BRAND – AND YOURSELF

In Chapter 3, I talked about how to find an investment Dragon and how Dragons are always hungry for their profits. Of course, they are. It's why they invested in your business. This means that eventually it will be payback time. But payback for the investor means *payout* for the business owner, so it is important to have a clear idea of the monetary value and potential of your brand.

When Richard Farleigh decided he wanted to sell his shares, less than 18 months after investing in the business, it was a big moment. I had to decide whether to buy back his shares. Would it be in the best interests of the business? It was an important decision and a significant investment, especially for a young start-up company. And, of course, I asked for advice, from both Peter Jones and my accountant.

One of the things that you, as an entrepreneur, need to tune into is *when* the right time to make a decision is. Was it the right time for Richard to sell? He made 700 per cent profit in less than two years – which is quite a killing by anyone's reckoning – so, yes, I think he felt it was the right time. Was it the right time for me to buy? Absolutely! I didn't want those shares to go to anyone else. I was Levi the Dragon-slayer again – coming in with my sword and reclaiming my territory!

Richard is a serial investor. He is a venture capitalist who wants to make sure he puts his money where it is likely to get the best return. He will recognize an opportunity, invest in something for a period of time, watch it grow, then when the moment is right he will take his profits and move on to his next investment. His judgement and timing are excellent.

Thanks to the progress we made in such a short time, I was able to pay him back eight times the amount that he had originally invested. Richard could see the potential for profit, whereas Peter was investing in Levi the man. Peter is in it for the longer term, and he had a different kind of vision. He could see a market for a whole range of Reggae Reggae products – and for 'brand Levi'. We work well together because we both have big plans, and with our joint experience we might just make it all happen.

Now, the company is worth a lot more compared with what it was worth when Richard bought the shares back. Is Richard kicking himself a little? He got a fantastic return on his investment, in cash. He later he told me that he focuses on the profits he makes, not the profits he doesn't make – the future growth of the business was still very speculative at the time when Richard sold his shares. He's happy – and so am I.

Peter Jones is more instrumental within the company than just as an investor. His contribution is not only that he invested in Roots Reggae Reggae Sauce Ltd, but in his mentoring: the advice that he ensures gets passed on to me, and his knowledge. I still have many lessons to learn from him and I am happy to admit that. He has many more years' business experience than I do. He knows me as a person, too, and has helped to guide me in the business world. These are skills that I will be able to pass on to others – the way it should be in business. There are times in life when we must not be afraid to make tough decisions that have a longer-lasting impact. And there are times when the true value means different things to different people; it may lie in the quick return for some and in the longer term picture for others.

In terms of your own planning, part of your overall business plan should take into account how you are going to get value from the business, as mentioned in Chapter 3. Are you in it for life – planning to get rich by making money faster than you are spending it? Is the business to be your family legacy? Or are you looking for an 'exit', and planning to fatten up the business and then sell it on? Assessing your personal goals and what value you want to achieve will have an impact on your planning for the business.

BRAND VALUES

"What's in a name?" as Shakespeare wrote. "That which we call a rose by any other name would smell as sweet." Well, Reggae Reggae Sauce would taste just as good whatever it was called – but in this case the name is part of the brand. I don't think it would have worked on such a large scale without that name. It is very important. It shouts music, food, and Caribbean loudly and instantly, and it is internationally recognizable for that reason.

Funnily enough, not everyone liked the name when I first thought of it. My friends said to me, "But, Levi, it is too black, too Jamaican, too Rasta." And I replied, "But that *is* me: I am black, I am Jamaican, I am Rasta. The sauce is associated with me – and so the brand is me, too!"

When you are naming your brand, think about the values you want your name and your look to represent, as well as who you are selling to. The price, the look, the quality, the USP – everything needs to be congruent and consistent with your own brand values.

One thing to remember is that different words mean different things in different cultures. One of our agents recently returned from a meeting in Australia to tell us that the word 'roots' means something a bit more crude and rude in their culture! So we will have to bear that in mind for our packaging if we launch out there. All of these details have to be considered and weighed up for importance.

A lot of companies nowadays do field research on potential names before they launch to make sure that the word appeals to their target market and does not have any unwanted connotations or associations. It is about putting personality in your business and making sure that your market understands your values and that you and your team represent those values – wherever you go.

PRODUCT VALUES

There are three basic product values that need to be consistent in your business: unit cost, customer service, and selling price. Make sure that they are either *all* high or *all* low, depending on sales volume.

- *Low* sales volume = *high* unit cost + *high* customer service + *high* selling price
- *High* sales volume = *low* unit cost + *low* customer service + *low* selling price

A supermarket ready meal will sell in high volume, so it can be priced low and produced relatively cheaply, with no need for individual customer service. A restaurant meal, on the other hand, will sell in low volume. Customers will pay a price per head that reflects the relatively high cost of buying good-quality ingredients in small volume. Customers will expect personal attention and high-quality service, too. It is the difference between selling a second-hand car or a high performance marque; an off-the-peg suit or bespoke tailoring from Savile Row. People expect to get what they pay for – and what they aspire to have.

It is a useful guideline to remember, because it can prevent you from making expensive mistakes. There is another reason, too: customers like consistency.

They will return to your business because they like what they have been getting and they know what to expect.

Selling is all about satisfying customers' needs and wants. Often a customer's wants will take priority over the needs, which is why a customer may be willing to splash out more money than planned on a pair of designer shoes they *want*, even though they really *need* a new pair of shoes for work.

Maintaining quality

Every industry has stock of some sort, and that stock represents money: your investment and potential profit. At my Papine Jerk restaurant, our investment is in our ingredients. Cooking for a menu is different from cooking at home. We can't simply add a couple of extra peppers to the cooking pot because we think the dish needs more flavour. There is a recipe to follow, which has been costed and accounted for. Nor do we want to overstock and waste fresh produce. Our profit is measured as much by what we throw away as by what we sell. When we serve our food to our customers, we want them to enjoy it and to recommend the experience to their friends. We know that each time they come back, they will expect their dish to taste the same.

KEEP YOUR INTEGRITY INTACT

Knowing what you want in business, as well as in life, is important. When we decided to move beyond marketing Reggae Reggae Sauce as a single product, into launching a whole range of products, it was done as part of a five-year plan. It was to build market share and, importantly, to establish the authenticity of the brand as specializing in Caribbean food.

As explained on page 195, that can sometimes mean turning down potentially lucrative and mass-market opportunities because it would send out the wrong message. Pizza, noodles, baked beans may be things that we would consider for the future, provided there was a fusion of flavours that made it worthwhile, but in the short term it would confuse our message. Further down the line we may look at merchandising, but that is not part of the plan right now, as it would not be in line with the brand values at the moment. The immediate objective for us is to keep building people's understanding and awareness of the brand.

If you allow yourself to get distracted, you may find yourself spending too much time on developing a product, idea, or customer that takes you away from your main area of focus. Always ask yourself:

- Will this opportunity take me closer to, or further away from, my long-term objective?
- What is the true cost in terms of time, investment, and development?
- Will it add to or distract from our core message?
- Will it deliver more of the kinds of customer we want in the future?

These questions are not so different from the ones that you ask yourself when faced with decisions that reflect on your value as a person.

PUTTING SOMETHING BACK

As you build in experience and you benefit from others' help
and knowledge, it is natural to want to share your know-
how and give something back. When I see a young person
making the wrong choices, I like to help them to change
their path in life if I can. I may be motivated by something
in them, or by the anguish I can see in their mother's eyes. It
reminds me of all I put my own mother through in my youth.

Young people need to learn to respect themselves.
They can't learn that only by being told about their potential,
although personal support is always a good thing – they need
to learn it for themselves. The key is to help people discover
and realize their own talent, then to help them to recognize
it. My role is often to say to a young person, "Look, this is your
talent. This could be your future. It's not about going out with
your friends and nicking stuff." If I can, I offer some practical
support to begin with – but as soon as they are ready I say,
"Right, now you support yourself."

> You need someone else to
> believe in you: to encourage
> you to live your dream.

It is important to go at the pace of the person you are trying
to help. Rather than saying, "You can do this, you can do that,"
I let the young person decide. They need time to make the
changes slowly and deliberately. Most of the time, all people
will ever need is some personal support. You need someone
else to believe in you: to encourage you to live your dream.

As with many other business owners, my business success was the result of overcoming adversity. That is what my *Dragons' Den* experience was really about. If you can overcome ferocious beasts and surmount seemingly insurmountable obstacles – like King Arthur did with his trusty sword, Excalibur – then you will learn the lessons and succeed in your business quest. For me, the myth of King Arthur slaying the dragons is more than a story. It is symbolic of my own path, which is why I use the story of *Dragons' Den* to explain my brand and promote my company.

Every business owner will have a different story to tell and a different way of promoting their brand. I have chosen to associate the story of my business with the story of how I built my brand. I have done some mad things in my life, but if you turn things around, and then move forward, you can make your life a success.

> Your business future is always rooted in your personal values and your experiences.

Your business future is always rooted in your personal values and your experiences. Despite my past mistakes, I try to live my life in a straight and honest way. I always believed that things would turn out well in the end, so when I got knocked back, I moved on. I was never afraid to go out there and pitch my business to people. The dream was always there and was always about success. If you know your value and stay true to yourself, your dreams will take you to where you want to go.

CHAPTER 10

BE IN IT FOR THE LONG TERM

Roots of success 10:
Be in it for the long term

> *"The race is not for the swift,*
> *nor the battle for the strong,*
> *but for those who can endure*
> *to the end."*

CARIBBEAN SAYING

I always say to people that they should plan for the long term. Keeping the bigger picture in mind from the outset is important because it makes you think on a larger scale, prepare better, and think harder about how committed you are to the path you have taken.

'Roots of success 1' was all about the level of passion and commitment you need to succeed. 'Roots of success 10' is about applying that commitment over time and distance, so you keep to your plan and build a profitable business that can be developed or sold. Commitment to the long term becomes ever more important the more successful you become – especially in those moments when you start to lose momentum, or are tempted to take your foot off the accelerator. Patience and commitment are your final Dragon-slaying weapons. They will keep you at the top of your game and your competitors at bay.

KEEP ON KEEPING GOING

Starting up in business is like being in a 100-metre race, where everything happens very fast. The two most important stages in the race are the start and the finish. In order to win, you need to have a good start that motivates you to get ahead of the pack to gain and maintain momentum all the way to the finish line.

Asafa Powell is a Jamaican athlete and one of the fastest runners in the world. I met him the day after he had run – and lost – an important race, and I asked him what had gone wrong after his excellent start. He told me he lost because he didn't focus right through to the finish line. He had what was wanted:

he got off the blocks fast, his head was in front, and it all looked promising. But just for a moment he lost concentration and in that second he lost momentum – at a crucial point in the race.

So getting off to a strong start is always crucial – but then you need to stay focused all the way to the end. If Asafa had kept the motivation going, he would have won, by a good length. The other lesson is that if you *do* get off to a bad start, it is even more important to sharpen up that focus so you have a chance to catch up and avoid losing.

World-class athletes become world-class partly because they have talent, but also because they work hard, daily, for years – usually under the close eye of a sporting coach or mentor. These days mentors are common in the business world, too. With as many as 500,000 new businesses starting up every year (according to the business information company Dun & Bradstreet), it makes good sense to get the best business advice you can, as early as you can – to give yourself the best chance of getting a head start in your own business race.

Building a business is not a sprint – it's a marathon. You need to stay aware of how far you have travelled and how far you still have to go, while monitoring and managing your resources. If you think only about your short-term goals, you may make the mistake of thinking you have arrived, when in fact you have hardly started. Or you may start worrying about what your competitors are doing, rather than being innovative and staying ahead of the market trend. By focusing on the long-term plan, you will know that each success is one step closer to the big picture, and that you still have a long way to go to complete the distance.

> Early success can lead to complacency. It is a time when you are vulnerable – because you are visible, and you have woken up your competitors to your achievements.

When you get your first taste of success, it is natural to feel your hunger wane slightly because you will feel that you've done it. You're there. You've got money in the bank. You can provide for your family. The excitement of the start-up phase is being gradually replaced by the challenge of the growth stage, which needs careful maintenance and management. From now on it becomes more about sustaining and developing, while laying the ground for the next development plan. This is the point at which many investors want to see the return on their investment – just as Richard Farleigh did with me. The fast growth is being replaced by something slower and steadier – hopefully for longer-term reward.

Maintaining success is always a different process to the start-up phase. It demands a different range of skills. That is why, when building your team (see Chapter 7), it is vital to bring on board people who have the skills you lack. They can help to build up the processes and the systems that a larger organization needs to succeed. Many people are motivated more by delivering a process than they are by building a business. They are there to safeguard your values and for continuity if and when you decide to expand or sell the business.

Early success can lead to complacency. It is a time when you are vulnerable – because you are visible, and you have woken up your competitors to your achievements. Your success may also blaze a trail for others, who could potentially take your place in the market.

If, on the other hand, you see your early success as the first stage of your five-year plan, you won't worry that others are trying to steal your thunder – because you will have anticipated it. You will be ready with new ideas and already onto the next stage of your plan. In those moments where your energy plateaus, pay extra attention to the money side of things. Ensuring you are in profit at the end of each working day will always keep you focused. At the Reggae Reggae Group we are nearing the final stage of our first five-year plan; and part of that plan is to plan ahead for the next five years – so we will keep on keeping going.

Once you have created your business it is all about moving on to the next level. It will come naturally, as you talk about business to others about business trends and opportunities and to your suppliers about the next deal and new promotional ideas.

BE IN IT FOR THE LONG TERM

Building a business is like walking through many doors to many rooms. You may get an impression of the whole building from the outside, but you can't envision what is inside until you open the doors. As each door opens, you work your way further in, and once you are familiar with the ground floor you will be ready to move up to the next level, and the next, and so on. You keep the whole picture in mind but you have to know how to deal with the stages as well: the start-up; getting funding; the marketing strategy. Each stage is an important door that will open and take you to the next level.

People ask me how they will be able to tell when it is time to expand. My answer is you will discover or develop opportunities. The right opportunity will come along, perhaps when you least expect it, but at a time when you will be ready for it. The door to that opportunity is usually being held open by a person who will help to direct your next course of action.

I was already selling my sauce on the market when I met Nadia Jones, who opened the door of opportunity in the form of networking and exhibitions. While I was at an exhibition, the television researcher from *Dragons' Den* opened the door of opportunity to investment from Peter Jones – who in turn opened the door of a major supermarket.

Looking back still further, my much-loved grandmother, Miriam, was the person who opened the door to my love of cooking, and my mother educated me in basic business skills and developed my love of learning. Importantly, there was also Theresa, the volunteer I met when I was in prison and who I never saw again – she showed me the door to a new life as Levi Roots, which released me from the trapdoor of my past mistakes.

Whatever stage you are at with your business, whether in a positive or negative state, the message I want to put across is that you can turn things around. From a negative, a positive can come; from a positive, there is a world of future possibilities. There are always lessons to be learned and benefits to be gained.

Welcome anything that encourages you to take your business up a notch. If a competitor opens up next door to you, take it as a sign that you are doing well enough to attract other businesses to the area. Ask yourself what you can do to raise your game and be one step ahead of the pack. Go back to basics: look at your customer profile, your pricing, what you are offering, the quality of your service, and so on. In every industry, you will find clusters of experts – even on the internet. It's the way of the business world. All you can do is strive to be the best and to remain true to your values, so that your customers become your brand ambassadors and tell everyone else about you.

Anything is possible in business – it is a matter of preparation and timing. You need to constantly ask yourself whether the time is right. It is not a matter of saying, "Never mind the business plan, I feel like diversifying into a new area now." You have to ask yourself, "When will it be possible for me to do that? What ground do I have to lay before I can include that in the business plan? What impact will there be on all the work we have done so far? Will it help or hinder our long-term success?" There is always a time span involved, and a moment for every movement.

THE MARKETPLACE IS ALWAYS CHANGING

A business will grow in line with the market for its goods or services, usually in five stages:

1 Start-up stage
2 Growth stage
3 Mature stage
4 Peak/decline
5 Exit

Each product line will develop through each of those stages, too, although the cycle happens more quickly. Product lines that are aimed at a fast-changing fashion or youth market may go from start-up to decline within a single season. The challenge for the business owner is to not over- or under-produce for the duration of the trend – while already being in the start-up phase for the next trend that will take its place.

Not every business has to be a trendsetter. There are those that make their mark by selling or developing classic goods and services that people rely upon. Nevertheless, most industries these days are being radically affected by changing technology and modes of buying and selling – as well as ever-more discerning consumers. If you want to stay successful for the long term, you will need to keep asking questions and to find out which changes will affect you and which won't.

INCREASING THE PACE

Success is not about making the first sale; it's about making repeat sales and building your customer base. That takes time to achieve, and it often comes more slowly than you anticipated. There is a saying in business that there is no such thing as overnight success. It is true, but there is a tipping point where everything suddenly comes together, and it starts to work: where suddenly it has the potential to grow and to get big.

There are three elements that you need to get right if you want your business to grow and develop:

• Develop a service or product that people want or need to buy.
• Find enough customers to buy your goods to ensure that you make a profit.
• Build a team of people capable of delivering your product or service to customers or clients.

Peter Jones always cautioned that there was a problem with scaling out a single product. The television exposure gave Reggae Reggae Sauce a novelty value, but we were concerned that it might be a one-hit wonder – which is one of the reasons we have been so aggressive with our product expansion. We have used the sauce as the flagship for all the other products that we have launched since. But the proof has been in the product. Our initial Reggae Reggae Sauce sold fantastically right from the outset, and the repeat sales are the proof of the quality of the product. Repeat sales tell you that you've arrived.

Within a few months of launching Reggae Reggae Sauce, people were saying to me, "Levi, what about Australia? What about America?" But then we had only one sauce, and it was far too early to think about expansion. Now, a few years down the line, we have nine different varieties of the sauce and more than ten different food products.

We were right to be patient and decide from the outset to build solidly and steadily. There is no point in rushing. We developed a marketing strategy that has made the brand come alive. There is now a feel-good factor that comes with using the brand – because we made it that way. That will make it easier to sell into new markets because it is something new and original. My approach was never to sit back and watch the sauce sell; it was always going to be important to connect myself to it. It's the combination of the sauce and the story together that is the secret of its success so far.

The early years of the Reggae Reggae Group have been about extending the brand as far as we can in the UK, while keeping the integrity of what Levi Roots is about. Sometimes the most difficult thing is to keep focused on the plan and on the dream, and not to allow yourself to get distracted by offers that are not congruent with the direction you are going in. Because our first five-year plan has been to build the brand here in the UK and only then to take it international, we are focused on building the brand into a strong market leader in Caribbean food. As we get closer to meeting our goal, we also get closer to the next stage. Levi Roots in America? Now that does sound good.

Entrepreneurs are impatient by nature. They want everything to happen now and fast. But just like the fable of the tortoise and the hare, it is the business owner with the clear game plan who wins in the end. Increasing the pace needs an ordered approach, with your whole team involved. It may also mean that you have to delegate more responsibility and have less immediate influence over daily decision-making. This doesn't mean however, that you have any less responsibility or control. Expansion puts greater demands on the business owner. You will need to make sure that the team keeps communicating with you, and with each other. This is no role for a shrinking violet. Now is the time to lead boldly from the front.

PLAN YOUR EXIT STRATEGY

There are two ways to build wealth from a business. The first is for the business to make you an income faster than you are spending it (hopefully over a long period of time) so that you can accumulate wealth. The second is to build a business, and then sell it for a large amount of money. Of course, the two ways are not alternatives: you can do the first and then the second. Business growth is all about opening the next door of opportunity – and one of the doors you should consider is the timing of your exit from the company. If you are planning an exit (and not planning to hand the business on to your heirs) you should think about your exit strategy as part of your first business plan, but even if you haven't written it down it should be in your head. Like every aspect of your business plan, you should keep reviewing it as your business grows. It is a constant reminder of why you want to make money and how far you want to take your venture, because most things have to have an end. Is your business in a sector where companies are bought and sold? Who would be likely to be interested in buying your business?

What type of prices are people paying for companies in your sector? Can the business survive without you (if it can't then it's not sellable). It will help you to stay focused, as every decision is taking you closer to your ultimate long-term goal, whether it is selling up and starting anew, or passing your company on to somebody else – or looking forward to the enjoyable early retirement that you have dreamed about and can't wait for!

It would be an enormous wrench to me to sell the Reggae Reggae companies. So much about the brand and the story is wrapped up with me personally. But from the moment it grew larger than the family kitchen, I have seen it as a business venture. At the back of my mind I know that one day I may have to make the dreaded decision to sell. By that point I hope the dream will have served its purpose.

BUILDING YOUR ENTERPRISE

Building a business and being enterprising really is about going boldly where no one has been before – you are the Captain of your own *Starship Enterprise*. My plans now as a person of enterprise are all about going into new territory and taking the model we have created into new fields.

This is when the benefit of all your experience becomes really useful. The cycle, and the battle, starts all over again – in new territory.

As we say in Jamaica, "The race is not for the swift, nor the battle for the strong" – but those who can endure will get to the end. Whatever the future holds, one thing I know for sure, I will always be Levi Roots – and I'll always have my music.

Imagine yourself sleeping and slumbering and dreaming. You're dreaming good things. Everything is working out well because you've stuck to your plan.

In the early stages of starting up your business the dream will be a motivating one – the memory of it will help you to stride forward. *But* it remains just as powerful once you start to make things happen.

When you wake up, if you feel as if you are *still* in your dream – because now you are living the dream and you have made it happen – that is when your dream becomes a fulfilling thing. Once you've had a taste of success, you will never want to let it go. It will make you want to work even harder, because you will want to keep a tight hold on all you have achieved.

When you start at shop-floor level and you work your way up to the boardroom, you really appreciate all that this represents. But if you ask any one of those people on the top floor, they will tell you how hard they still have to work to stay there – even if it *is* their own company. If someone on the board or a major shareholder thinks you are slouching a bit too much in that boardroom chair, and that you are no longer of value to the company, they will have the power to help you step down. It shows that you still have to keep your foot on that pedal because you've got used to being at your new level, and you don't want to start going back down again. Building success gives you the will and the opportunity to develop, and even more opportunities will start to open up.

REMEMBER THE ROOTS OF SUCCESS

1 Feel the power of the p-word – passion

Your passion is the driving force behind your business. Tune in to what truly motivates you and you will also discover the unique selling point for your business. It is the key that sets you apart from the rest of the pack. Your USP represents your Unique Self and your Passion.

2 Know your market – and never stop networking

It's important to know your market niche: where your product or service lies in relation to your competitors and within the broader marketplace. Connecting with others in the industry is the best way to keep up to date with trends and opportunities.

3 The plan is your key to success

Never start up in business without a plan. It is the backbone of everything you will go on to achieve. It is your progress marker and your motivator. It is also the document that will attract others to invest in your venture.

4 Find yourself a mentor

No entrepreneur is an island. You can't possibly know everything, and you can never know too much. Learning from those who have more experience is the most effective way to avoid making unnecessary mistakes and to develop your business wisely.

5 Make yourself and your business special

Your branding and marketing plan are the keys to your business growth. Standing out from the crowd and constantly staying ahead of the market trend are perhaps the most challenging aspects of running your business. Attracting loyal customers who want to be associated with what you and your product or service represents will help your brand's reputation to grow.

6 Never be afraid to make mistakes

Setting up in business is always a calculated risk, but you can never learn, develop, or become a success without making a few mistakes along the way. Mistakes are the lessons you need to learn before you can become successful. Take the feedback from the down times then move on.

7 Surround yourself with like-minded people

Your business is only as good as the weakest person in your team. Select people who can offer the right skills you need for the job, then make sure they are inspired to give all of their best and feel appreciated. Remember that not everyone goes at the same pace as you – allow others to find their own rhythm.

8 Focus on finance

All businesses need to make money. At the end of the day, a profit is the only acceptable result. Make sure you pay attention to the financial detail as well as the big picture. Overspending or undercharging on the small things can have a big long-term effect. Manage your cash flow every day.

9 Stay true to your values

You are your business and your business is a part of you. Never forget that. The more people that are involved in all you are striving for, the more voices there will be who want to shape your views. Always listen, then make up your own mind. Sometimes you will need to walk away from a potentially lucrative deal or offer because it does not fit with what you stand for and what you want to offer.

10 Be in it for the long term

Business growth can only happen over time. There is a process that has to unfold.

It is important to be yourself in business and to believe in what you do. If you put your personality into your business and do the best you can, you will make your business special. I think that's the best lesson I can give to anybody. After that, it is all about perseverance: having a plan, always focusing on that plan, and having loads of passion for it. No one is born an entrepreneur - I certainly wasn't. But everyone has the choice to turn themselves into an entrepreneur, if they want to. You *can* do it too if you *really* want to.

> No one is born an entrepreneur - I certainly wasn't. I turned myself into an entrepreneur. You can do it too if you *really* want to.

FURTHER READING

You can never read too much about how to run a business, and luckily there are more resources than ever before available to entrepreneurs. You can find information everywhere, for example, on newspapers' financial pages, in the *Financial Times*, on TV business programmes, on YouTube, in business books, and in autobiographies of successful people. The following are just a few that I can recommend:

Tycoon – **Peter Jones**

The essential guide from the man himself. The nearest you will get to having Peter as your mentor unless he invests in you on *Dragons' Den* or you sign up for his National Enterprise Academy.

100 Secret Strategies for Successful Investing – **Richard Farleigh**

I was fortunate that Richard shared some of his secrets with me when we set up my company.

Common Sense Rules – **Deborah Meaden**

Deborah's down-to-earth advice is drawn from the lessons she has learned during the course of running her own companies.

Dragons' Den Start Your Own Business
Dragons' Den The Perfect Pitch
Dragons' Den Grow Your Business

These books are written by industry experts, and they will give you all the nitty-gritty and inside information you need to starting your own business.

Enter the Dragon – **Theo Paphitis**

Theo takes readers behind the scenes of *Dragons' Den* and provides a masterclass in business methods.

The Real Deal – **James Caan**

James started life with nothing, and his story shows just how far it is possible for a Dragon to go in business.

Wake Up and Change Your Life – **Duncan Bannatyne**

Duncan didn't want to try a taste of Reggae Reggae Sauce – but he knows about running businesses, and he has written several books. This is the one that will wake you up to the reality of starting one up.

What's Your Bright Idea? – **Tim Campbell and Paul Humphries**

Tim Campbell is doing a lot of great work with business start-ups, and this book tells you his approach.

FURTHER RESOURCES

This is just a small handful of the organizations and resources that new enterprises have at their fingertips in the UK today. Use the internet to its full capacity to find and connect with like-minded people who can help you to build your business and learn new skills. If you are aiming to target customers in your local area, it is a very good idea to network with other local business owners and start-ups, and to be connected to your local business community.

WHERE TO ASK FOR ADVICE

Bright Ideas Trust

www.brightideastrust.com
Founded by my good friend Tim Campbell, the first winner of the TV programme *The Apprentice* in the UK, the Bright Ideas Trust is managed by a team of experienced business entrepreneurs who provide a package of advice to young people aged 16–30 who are currently not in employment and who want to start a business.

Business Link

www.businesslink.gov.uk
The Business Link website will give you a whole array of useful advice, including links to sample business plans and business plan templates. Some of them are more complicated than will be necessary for your company. Keep yours clear and simple.

The Department of Business Industry and Skills (BIS)

www.bis.gov.uk
A new government department with a large team and a £21 billion budget dedicated to helping education, training and business. The Enterprise Finance Guarantee scheme (EFG) has been set up to help support new businesses with loan finance.

GLE

www.gle.co.uk
Greater London Enterprise is where the Reggae Reggae Sauce business began. Its advice is freely given. There are several branches across London.

James Caan's Entrepreneurs' Business Academy

www.the-eba.com
Founded with Bev James, James Caan's EBA provides business mentoring support on a payment basis to existing companies and start-ups.

Peter Jones

www.peterjones.tv
Peter has put together a whole range of resources for start-up companies, so you can get off to a bright start.

Peter Jones's National Enterprise Academy

www.thenea.org

Part of the National Skills Academy, Peter's academy was started in 2005 in order to invest in the next generation of UK entrepreneurs. He has a mission to change the 'Can I?' mentality of young entrepreneurs into more of a positive 'I can' mind-set.

Prime Business Club

www.primebusinessclub.com

A website aimed at 'olderpreneurs' who are starting a business at 50+.

PRIME (The Prince's Initiative for Mature Enterprise)

www.primeinitiative.co.uk

A charity focused on helping to fund start-up businesses for the over-50s.

The Prince's Trust

www.princes-trust.org.uk

A youth trust that focuses on changing people's lives. Its youth enterprise programme helps young unemployed people aged 18–30 to work out whether their business ideas are viable.

Startups

www.startups.co.uk

A useful online resource offering news and advice for business start-ups, run by Crimson Business Ltd.

GETTING SET UP IN BUSINESS

Companies House

www.companieshouse.gov.uk

Contact centre:

+44 (0)303 1234 500

Companies House has three main functions: to incorporate and dissolve limited companies; to examine and store company information that has been submitted in line with the Companies Act and related legislation; and to make this information available to the public.

Health and Safety Executive

www.hse.gov.uk

Ask an expert: 0845 345 0055

The role of the HSE is to protect people's health and safety in the workplace. It has a lot of influence over how things should be done and makes sure that proper controls are in place. Get in touch for advice before you set up your premises.

HM Revenue & Customs

www.hmrc.gov.uk

Newly self-employed helpline: 0845 915 4515

New employer helpline: 0845 607 0143

The HMRC ensures that the correct amount of tax is paid by individuals and businesses, and at the right time. Its advisors are extremely helpful, and the website offers a range of contacts, depending on the nature and type of enquiry.

Investors in People
www.investorsinpeople.co.uk
An organization that sets up structures for monitoring and improving performance and productivity in the workplace.

National Business Register Plc
www.start.biz
Includes clear and free information about starting up and registering company details, complete with video segments. There are fees payable for registration.

ROUTES TO FINANCE
The British Business Angels Association (BBAA)
www.bbaa.org.uk
The only national trade association dedicated to promoting angel investing and supporting early-stage investment in the UK.

The British Private Equity & Venture Capital Association
www.bvca.co.uk
Its aim is to aid understanding, clarity, and transparency around the activities of its members and to promote their industry.

Capital for Enterprise
www.capitalforenterprise.gov.uk
CfEL is the government's centre of expertise for SME (small and medium-sized enterprise) funding. Its expert team creates funding schemes for small businesses.

GrantsNet
www.grantsnet.co.uk
A searchable database that provides information on grants, loans, and funding schemes.

NFEA
www.nfea.com
The national enterprise network. Members are drawn from local enterprise agencies. Their role is to help people to set up and run their own business.

RISK MANAGEMENT
European Patent Office
www.epo.org
Provides a uniform application procedure for individual inventors and companies seeking patent protection in up to 40 European countries.

Intellectual Property Office
www.ipo.gov.uk
Enquiries: 0845 950 0505
The IPO is the official government body responsible for advising on and granting intellectual property rights in the UK. It is your starting point for information relating to patents, trademarks, design, and copyright.

GETTING CONNECTED

British Chambers of Commerce (BCC)

www.britishchambers.org.uk
www.thebusiness-startup.co.uk
There is a chamber of commerce in every county in Britain. BCC is a bridge between local businesses and local government. It runs a related website that offers valuable information for business start-ups.

Institute of Directors

www.iod.com
Enquiries: 020 7766 8866
Most industries have a business club or organization that provides a useful forum for networking and other resources. The IoD has a network of locations across most major cities in the UK. Club membership can be expensive, though, so only join one if you can see what the return would be on your investment.

USEFUL SOURCES

BBC

www.bbc.co.uk/news/business
A useful place to catch up on business and finance news in the UK and around the world.

Business Startup – the Business Show

www.bstartup.com
The Business Startup Show is where it all started for me, and now I return as a speaker whenever my schedule allows. There are seminars and talks on every topic, given by people who have already made it. It is great for networking – and is free.

Global Enterprise Week

www.gew.org.uk
A not-for-profit organization that helps people to improve their business skills and get support for their ideas.

HM Government

Each political party has an MP who represents business interests. The main three party websites are:
The Conservative Party:
www.conservatives.com
The Labour Party:
www.labour.org.uk
The Liberal Democrats:
www.libdems.org.uk
Lobby your MP for better support for businesses, and get onto your mayor and local councillors, too.

VideoJug

www.videojug.com/tag/small-business
There are some useful tips in the videos posted by professional business people in the small business section of the VideoJug website. You will find guidance on everything from setting up an invoice system to giving a presentation.

YouTube
www.youtube.co.uk
Enter the name of any entrepreneur or business guru you can think of, and some nuggets of spoken wisdom will appear in front of your eyes. Inspiration is only ever a click away. Try 'Levi Roots business' for starters, and you won't go far wrong!

WHERE TO FIND AN ACCOUNTANT

Always get a personal recommendation if you can. The following associations can provide details of accountants in your area.

The Association of Chartered Certified Accountants (ACCA)
www.accaglobal.com

Chartered Institute of Management Accountants (CIMA)
www.cimaglobal.com

The Institute of Chartered Accountants in England and Wales (ICAEW)
www.icaewfirms.co.uk

The Institute of Chartered Accountants of Scotland (ICAS)
www.icas.org.uk

The Institute of Chartered Accountants in Ireland (ICAI)
www.icai.ie

WHERE TO FIND LEGAL ADVICE

Solicitors are listed in every phone book – but don't just take pot luck. Ask those you know for a recommendation. And if you don't know anyone who would know, ask someone you respect in business for their advice.

The Chartered Institute of Patent Attorneys
www.cipa.org.uk
Provides advice on protecting designs, copyright, trademarks, and domain names.

The Institute of Trade Mark Attorneys
www.itma.org.uk
Offers advice on trademarks and the law.

The Law Society of England and Wales
www.lawsociety.org.uk
Helps, protects, and promotes solicitors in England and Wales.

The Law Society of Scotland
www.lawscot.org.uk
Represents, supports, and regulates solicitors in Scotland.

WHERE TO FIND HELP WITH EMPLOYMENT LAW

Business Link will be very helpful in this area, but you can also try:

The Chartered Institute of Personnel and Development (CIPD)

www.cipd.co.uk
Offers professional advice to personnel professionals on the management and development of people.

Directgov

www.direct.gov.uk
The website of the UK government provides information and contacts for all aspects of British law and politics.

LIST OF CONTRIBUTORS

Zaion Graham

Zaion is my eldest son and manager of the Papine Jerk Centre in Battersea, London.

Nadia Jones

Nadia has been a business advisor and mentor for more than 15 years, mainly working with young disadvantaged and long-term unemployed clients to help them develop business ideas, write business plans, attract funding, and establish viable sustainable businesses. As a business advisor for creative industries with GLE oneLondon in Brixton, she worked with many creative clients, including me. She worked for the Prince's Trust as a Business Development Manager in Croydon and Bromley, establishing its business programme for the 18–30 age group. Nadia started her career in the fashion and retail industry working on the shop floor, in buying offices, and in a production department.

Peter Jones CBE

One of Britain's best-known entrepreneurs and investors, Peter is familiar to many for his role on *Dragons' Den*. He set up his first company at the age of 17 and started his first major business aged 19. Since that time he has built a £200 million business and is owner, chairman, and chief executive of a large portfolio of businesses. He is chairman of Enterprise UK and has recently launched his own National Enterprise Academy teaching entrepreneurship to young people aged 16–19.

Shah Khan

Shah Khan is marketing manager for Levi Roots' Reggae Reggae brand at AB Foods. He has managed a number of leading food and drink brands and is a graduate Cass Business School, London.

Teja Picton Howell

Teja is a solicitor with over 25 years' experience of UK and international corporate transactions. He was founder of Picton Howell solicitors and international lawyers. His legal practice ranges from multinational corporations, banks and investment funds to smaller owner managed companies. He particularly enjoys working with fast growing, entrepreneurial businesses, helping to steer them on their paths to profitability and building capital value.

Andrew Subramaniam

Andrew is a chartered accountant and specializes in advising authors, journalists, musicians, television personalities, and other media individuals, many of whom are household names. He joined HW Fisher & Company (www.hwfisher.co.uk) as an audit trainee in 1991. Since qualifying as a chartered accountant, he has held a number of positions within the firm and has been a partner for a number of years.

AUTHOR'S ACKNOWLEDGEMENTS

I would like to thank Peter Jones; Teja Picton Howell; Shah Khan; Andrew Subramaniam; John Eastaff; Zaion Graham and the team at Papine Jerk Centre; Nadia Jones; Rodney Levine-Boatang and Natasha Eggough at 100 Acres; Borra Garson and Emma Hughes at Deborah McKenna; Denise Bates, Sybella Stephens and the team at Mitchell Beazley.

PUBLISHER'S ACKNOWLEDGEMENTS

The publisher would like to thank Sarah Sutton, Alexandra Rutter and Keith King

INDEX